2 3 JUN 2009

For

D1427797

Succeed at psychometric testing

PRACTICE TESTS FOR
NUMERICAL
REASONING
ADVANCED LEVEL

New edition

For Reference Only

Succeed at psychometric testing

PRACTICE TESTS FOR
NUMERICAL
REASONING

ADVANCED LEVEL

Bernice Walmsley

HODDER
EDUCATION
PART OF HACHETTE UK

New edition

The publisher has used its best endeavours to ensure that the URLs for external websites referred to in this book are correct and active at the time of going to press. However, the publisher and the author have no responsibility for the websites and can make no guarantee that the site will remain live or that the content will remain relevant, decent or appropriate.

Orders: please contact Bookpoint Ltd, 130 Milton Park, Abingdon, Oxon OX14 4SB. Telephone: (44) 01235 827720. Fax: (44) 01235 400454. Lines are open from 9.00–5.00, Monday to Saturday, with a 24-hour message answering service. You can also order through our website www.hoddereducation.co.uk.

British Library Cataloguing in Publication Data
A catalogue record for this title is available from the British Library.

ISBN: 978 0 340 96927 4

First Published 2004
Second edition 2008
Impression number   10 9 8 7 6 5 4 3
Year   2012 2011 2010 2009

Copyright © 2004, 2008 Bernice Walmsley

Typeset by Servis Filmsetting Ltd, Stockport, Cheshire.
Printed in Great Britain for Hodder Education, part of Hachette UK, 338 Euston Road, London NW1 3BH by CPI Cox & Wyman, Reading, Berkshire, RG1 8EX.

Hachette UK's policy is to use papers that are natural, renewable and recyclable products and made from wood grown in sustainable forests. The logging and manufacturing processes are expected to conform to the environmental regulations of the country of origin.

CONTENTS

ACKNOWLEDGEMENTS

With thanks to SHL, for permission to reproduce the following material: Test 1, Questions 22–30; Test 3, Questions 11–14 and Figures 2.1 and 2.2; Test 3, Questions 16–19 and Table 2.3 and Figure 2.3.

FOREWORD

Should anyone tell you that a psychometric test will give an accurate indication of your level of intelligence, don't pay too much attention. It isn't necessarily true.

The credibility of the global psychometric testing industry rests on the belief of employers that a psychometric test will yield accurate and reliable data about a candidate's ability. Busy employers buy into the notion that a psychometric test will swiftly eliminate all the unsuitable candidates and deliver up only the best, brightest and most able candidates to the interview stage.

What is not widely known is that it is perfectly possibly for a candidate to drastically improve their own psychometric score by adopting a methodical approach to test preparation. The purpose of the *Succeed at Psychometric Testing* series is to provide you with the necessary tools for this purpose.

It is useful to know that a candidate's ability to perform well in a psychometric test is determined by a wide range of factors, aside from the difficulty of the questions in the test. External factors include the test environment and the professionalism of the test administrator; internal factors relate to the candidate's confidence level on the day, the amount of previous test practice the candidate has and the candidate's self-belief that they will succeed. While you cannot always control the external factors, you can manage many of the internal factors.

A common complaint from test takers is the lack of practice material available to them. The titles in the *Succeed at Psychometric Testing* series address this gap and the series is designed with you, the test taker in mind. The content focuses on practice and explanations rather than on the theory and science. The authors are all experienced test takers and understand the benefits of thorough test preparation. They have prepared the content with the test taker's priorities in mind. Research has shown us that test takers don't have much notice of their test, so they need lots of practice, right now, in an environment that simulates the real test as closely as possible.

In all the research for this series, I have met only one person who likes – or rather, doesn't mind – taking psychometric tests. You are not alone. This person is a highly successful and senior manager in the NHS and she has taken psychometric tests for many of the promotions for which she has applied. Her attitude to the process is sanguine: 'I have to do it, I can't get out of it and I want the promotion so I might as well get on with it.' She always does well. A positive mental attitude is absolutely crucial in preparing yourself for your upcoming test and will undoubtedly help you on the day. If you spend time practising beforehand and become familiar with the format of the test, you are already in charge of some of the factors that deter other candidates on the day.

It's worth bearing in mind that the skills you develop in test preparation will be useful to you in your everyday life and in your new job. For many people, test preparation is not the most joyful way to spend free time, but know that by doing so, you are not wasting your time.

The *Succeed at Psychometric Testing* series covers the whole spectrum of skills and tests presented by the major test publishers and will help you prepare for your numerical, verbal, logical, abstract and diagrammatic reasoning tests. The series now also includes a title on personality testing. This new title will help you understand the role that personality testing plays in both the recruitment process and explains how such tests can also help you to identify areas of work to which you, personally, are most suited. The structure of each title is designed to help you to mark your practice tests quickly and find an expert's explanation to the questions you have found difficult.

If you don't attain your best score at your first attempt, don't give up. Book yourself in to retake the test in a couple of months, go away and practise the tests again. Psychometric scores are not absolute and with practice, you can improve your score.

Good luck! Let us know how you get on.

Heidi Smith, Series Editor
educationenquiries@hodder.co.uk

Other titles in the series:

CHAPTER ONE
INTRODUCTION

WHO SHOULD READ THIS BOOK

This book is aimed at anyone of graduate and/or management level who may have to take psychometric tests in the near future. It may be that you have been called for a job interview and have heard that there will be a series of tests. You may even have been told specifically that you will be subjected to 'Psychometric Testing' and that this will include testing of your numerical skills. Or you may be applying for promotion and it has been mentioned that numerical ability will be important. Or you may be hoping to be accepted on a management development programme in your company and know that tests will be used to select the most appropriate candidates from those who have applied. Yet another example of people who would find the practice involved in this book useful is the candidate for the Civil Service who may be dreading their forthcoming UK Civil Service Fast Stream Qualifying Tests. (These tests feature a type of question based upon algebra for which it can be difficult to find practice material.) Whatever your situation, for most people the prospect of being tested is not a pleasant one.

But, make no mistake, it is possible to improve your score. Of course, the people who devise and publish these tests and the people who administer them don't publicise this fact. Publishers' sales depend on their clients believing that the results of the tests will guide them to the best candidates for the jobs on offer. The mystique of tests must be maintained.

There is no doubt that psychometric testing is not as straightforward as measuring your height or weight – your score may well change from day to day. Lots of factors will affect your performance including lack of confidence, stress, the conditions in the testing venue and so on, so your test score on the day can only ever be an indication or estimation of your ability. This fact is sometimes forgotten and tests given greater credibility than perhaps they deserve but they are certainly something that you can prepare for and by doing so improve your performance. With practice you can get rid of some of the stress and lack of confidence and other barriers to success. In the next section we'll look at five factors that can affect your score on the day.

If you have been out of the education system for some years or you have been studying for a degree that has not demanded much use of the numerical skills you learned at school, you may have a dislike – or even a fear – of numbers. However, numerical reasoning tests are certainly something that you can prepare for and this preparation will improve your performance. Testing yourself on actual examples of the types of test you will encounter is vital. Then, and only then, can you assess where your efforts to improve need to be focused.

HOW TO IMPROVE YOUR SCORE

Most graduates and applicants for jobs at a senior level (the people at whom this book is aimed) are not in any way innumerate. If they have problems with numerical tests, it is more likely to be due to short comings in speed and accuracy or a lack of recent use of the vital skills rather than to a lack of ability.

The numerical knowledge that you will need to perform well in these tests is the maths you learned at school. It might be that you need a quick refresher course, but just as useful will be the sort of practice contained in this book and the explanations that accompany the answers to the questions. It is perfectly possible to improve your score by your own efforts. The aims of this book are therefore twofold – to improve your performance in numerical tests by providing you with the practice you need and also to help you to lessen the impact of the factors that will affect your chances of success.

Before we go on to the main body of this book – the practice and explanations of mathematical problems – let's look at the factors that may affect your chances of success:

BELIEF IN YOUR ABILITY

This is about self-confidence. Research shows that a high expectation of success can be an important factor in getting a higher score. If you can get to the point where you know that you are well prepared and competent then you will improve your chances of success. This is because feeling confident increases the quantity of the type of hormones in your bloodstream that help you to focus. If, on the other hand, you're convinced that you will fail, then different hormones will make you anxious and less able to focus.

FAMILIARITY

Extensive evidence of the impact of coaching and practice on performance in a variety of examinations shows that it improves performance dramatically. It may be that you have been sent some practice material by the people who will be administering your test. Inevitably, this will not involve many questions but it will show you what sort of questions you will have to deal with and you will be able to concentrate on the timed tests in this book that equate to the material received. Whatever the focus of the particular test that you are taking, the large quantity of practice questions in this book will certainly give you the advantage of familiarity.

SPEED

Speed rather than accuracy is what is most important in most of the psychometric tests that you will take – although it's worth saying here that wild guesses are very rarely useful. Speed is significant because tests are almost always based simply on the number you get right in a fixed amount of time and then your score is compared with a similar group of test-takers. Because of the way scores are evaluated and compared with others, only a slight improvement in your performance will dramatically improve your final evaluation. So, the more questions you answer the more chance you have of getting that vital extra point or two.

In view of the need for speed, the best advice is:

- Always answer as many questions as possible.
- Go for speed not accuracy – but concentration is still essential.
- Never spend too much time on any one question.

UNDERSTANDING

It is vital that you understand completely what is required of you in the test. You will not get a good score if you do not follow instructions and understand precisely what you are meant to do. For this reason it is worth practising the various types of test and, of course, reading the instructions carefully.

ENVIRONMENT

This is an element of the tests over which you have little control. Ideally, tests should be conducted in a quiet, comfortable area but it is not unknown for tests to be given in office corridors, open plan offices or 'spare' offices where the heating has been turned off or the phone keeps ringing. Practising at home may be good preparation for this eventuality as life will still go on around you while you are practising.

Having said that, the correct environment is certainly a factor in your getting the best score of which you are capable, so do not be afraid to complain if things are not right – it is likely that serious problems will be taken into account when assessing your performance if they are brought to the attention of the test administrator.

WHAT IS NUMERICAL REASONING?

Numerical reasoning is the ability to deal with numbers and to get useful information from them. When your aptitude in this area is being tested you will have to show that you can add, subtract, divide and multiply as well as work with fractions, percentages and ratios and probably also show your understanding of data in charts, tables and graphs. Sometimes, particularly in the UK Civil Service Fast Stream Qualifying Tests, you will also need an understanding of basic algebra. These are all skills that you will have been taught at school. Practice will help you to remember them.

WHY TEST NUMERICAL REASONING?

There is a common belief that, unless you are an accountant or working in a bank, then you do not need to have an aptitude for numbers. This is absolutely not the case. Just think for a moment about the real business world – here are just a few examples:

- Volume discounts
- Minimum order values
- Pension calculations
- Engineering projects
- Technical specifications
- Budgets and targets

The examples of situations in which you need to be able to work with numbers are endless. And do not fall into the trap of thinking that, in this world where calculators are commonplace or where we have computers to help, you do not need to be able to work things out in your head. What about that sales manager who needs to get an idea of what price she will accept in the middle of complex negotiations? Or the businessman receiving a batch of invoices – he could save a lot of time by knowing at a glance that the invoices are added up correctly. In the real world numbers are everywhere so we need to be able to use them quickly and accurately and our prospective employers will be looking for this ability.

From an employer's point of view, interviewing and taking on staff is an expensive and risky business. There are a number of ways in which aptitude testing can help an employer:

- Where a company has received a large number of applicants, tests can whittle down the number to a more manageable and cost effective level for interviewing.

- Tests can be combined with other selection procedures to enable the employer to make better recruitment decisions.

- Tests are much less subjective than interviews alone – this is better for the employer and for the interviewees.

- Better decisions at this stage will result in a lower staff turnover.

- Selecting the right employees will reduce employee induction costs or wasted training.

- Employing the right people will lead to a reduction in the possibility of damage being done to a business by an incompetent member of staff.

- CVs are notoriously unreliable. Anyone can declare that they are numerate – tests will show whether or not this is actually true.

With these reasons in mind, we can see that an employer would be well advised to find a more efficient way of selecting staff than interviews alone. Mistakes in recruitment are expensive. Employers frequently use aptitude tests as an additional tool to help with their decision making – especially if they have a large number of applicants.

WHAT SORTS OF TESTS WILL YOU BE GIVEN?

The sets of aptitude tests given by employers may include ones to assess a variety of things such as your verbal reasoning or diagrammatic reasoning. However, our aim in this book is to concentrate on numerical reasoning.

Numerical reasoning tests will be timed and you will have to work quickly – but accurately. You will be told whether or not the use of calculators is permissible and whether or not you are allowed to write on the question papers. The questions quite often have multiple-choice answers and you will be told how to indicate your answers. This may be by ticking or putting a cross in a space or sometimes by shading in a square or circle on the answer paper. This latter method is to facilitate either computer marking or marking using a template in the case of large numbers of people taking the test. Whatever the instructions, it is vital that you follow them to the letter. If you are told to indicate your answer with a tick for example, do not put a cross. The person marking the test could possibly interpret this as your having deleted your answer to that question.

There are a number of different types of question at this level that can be used to assess your aptitude for numbers:

- General mathematical – including word problems, number sequences and basic arithmetic
- Tests based on tabulated data, graphs and charts
- Quantitative relations – i.e. useful practice for the UK Civil Service Fast Stream Qualifying Tests

Each of these test types is intended to discover a different aspect of your ability to use numbers.

At this point, it will be helpful to explain the layout of the questions, answers and explanations included in this book. As you will see, there will be a chapter of timed tests giving you plenty of practice and so that you can simulate test conditions. After this there will be a chapter devoted to explanations of the answers. This will include plenty of advice as to how you can tackle the questions and specific problems to look out for. You should note the correct answers and, even if you have got that one right, read the accompanying explanation. This is where the common pitfalls will be demonstrated and tips given on how to avoid them. Do not worry if you find at this point that you have made an elementary mistake – almost everyone does. It is highly unlikely that you will get every single answer correct. Reading the explanations will highlight the possible stumbling blocks.

HOW TO USE THIS BOOK

As an introduction, we will now look in a little more detail at the different types of questions:

1 GENERAL MATHEMATICAL

The first two timed tests will contain a variety of questions, including simple arithmetical tests, aimed at evaluating your ability to use the four basic operations of addition, subtraction, division and multiplication, alongside your understanding of numbers used in different formats. These formats include percentages, fractions and decimals and will take a variety of forms – straightforward calculations, number sequences and word problems.

As you can see, this section covers an enormous variety of questions. It will be useful here to look at some of these types. The tests in the main part of this book are timed and the answers and explanations – including tips on how to tackle the questions and some pitfalls to avoid related to the specific questions – will be contained in a chapter separate from the questions so that you will be able to test yourself in a situation as close to the actual test conditions as possible. However, as an introduction to the types of questions, we will quickly run through the whole question/answer/explanation process. Here are a few examples of the type of question you may encounter when you sit a real test of this sort:

ARITHMETIC

These are usually the most basic of the types of numerical reasoning test questions that will be encountered. They are based on arithmetical operations that most people will have learned and used throughout their school life. However, without day-to-day use, we all soon become less proficient at using these skills. You may have been studying a degree subject that does not emphasise numeracy or doing a job where you are using a calculator whenever figures are involved so that you do not think about numbers very much. This section is where practice might produce the most dramatic improvements.

Questions

1 29333 + 434 + 17 = ?

2 6234 − 5979 = ?

3 25 × 321 = ?

4 616 ÷ 22 = ?

Answers

1 29784

2 255

3 8025

4 28

Explanations

There are not usually any pitfalls associated with straightforward arithmetic questions like this. Work through the questions methodically and as quickly as you can without sacrificing accuracy. The more you do this type of question, the quicker you will get. With questions involving numbers of this size you will usually be either allowed to use a calculator or to use a piece of paper for rough workings. Most people would not be able to do long division calculations in their head – so don't panic.

It cannot be overstated – practice can make a great deal of difference here. If you find that you struggle with this type of question, a basic book on arithmetic, added to plenty of practice will help. The knowledge to answer these questions will have been gained at school and bringing yourself up to speed on this should be a priority if you have problems in this area.

PERCENTAGES, FRACTIONS AND DECIMALS

Although the questions in this section may seem varied and unrelated, the way in which the calculations work is very similar. Percentages are closely related to fractions in that percentages are expressed in parts of one hundred e.g. 50% is 50 parts of one hundred and could also be expressed as $\frac{50}{100}$ or $\frac{1}{2}$, that is one half. Decimals are also closely connected – the decimal point separates the whole number from the decimal fraction. You may also encounter ratio calculations in this section.

As you can see, the questions in this section have a selection of answers supplied for you to choose from. When you are given a multiple choice like this, usually only one answer will be correct. This may sometimes give you the opportunity to save time by estimating your answer and eliminating the obviously incorrect answers from those suggested rather than working out your exact answer. You can treat the multiple-choice answers as a list of suggestions.

A word of warning at this point. Do not guess at random. Some tests penalise this via the scoring system and there may be deductions for wrong or unanswered questions.

One more thing to be aware of is that, in dealing with multiple-choice questions, it is especially important to take notice of the instructions you will be given on how to indicate your answer. There are a variety of ways that test compilers require you to complete the tests. You may be required to indicate with a cross or a tick – be warned that they are not interchangeable. You are asking for a low score if you ignore instructions of this type.

Questions

1 45% of £15 =?

    a £7.75   **b** £5.00   **c** £6.75   **d** £5.75   **e** £6.25

2 $9\frac{5}{8} - 6\frac{1}{4}$ =?

    a $4\frac{1}{2}$ **b** $3\frac{3}{8}$ **c** 2   **d** $3\frac{1}{4}$ **e** $3\frac{5}{8}$

3 5.35 + 14.9 − 2.33 =?

    a 22.58   **b** 21   **c** 18.0   **d** 17.92   **e** 18.82

Answers

1 **c** £6.75

2 **b** $3\frac{3}{8}$

3 **d** 17.92

Explanations

1 Answer **c** £6.75 is correct. Remember that 45 per cent is the same as $\frac{45}{100}$ ths and that there are a number of ways that you can tackle this sort of question. For example, you could divide £15.00 by 100 then multiply by 45 or you could work out work out 45% of £10 then multiply by 1.5 (i.e. £10 + half of £10) — whichever you find easiest. The calculation is: $\frac{45}{100} \times 15$

2 Answer **b** $3\frac{3}{8}$ is correct. As with most fraction calculations, you need to find the common denominator (a denominator is the number at the bottom of the fraction so a common denominator is one into which all the denominators will divide). In this case it is 8, as both 8 and 4 – the two denominators – will go into this. After expressing the calculation using the common denominator, it will be relatively easy to find your answer, i.e. $9\frac{5}{8} - 6\frac{2}{8} = 3\frac{3}{8}$.

3 Answer **d** 17.92 is correct. Probably the only place where you may go wrong – whether because you are hurrying or because you are not familiar with decimals – is in getting the decimal point in the wrong place. To overcome this, you must be extremely careful to keep everything lined up, that is the decimal point directly under the one above and all the figures in their equivalent places. Other than this, a calculation like this one is just the same as a simple addition followed by a simple subtraction.

WORD PROBLEMS

Word problems of this sort are designed to test not only your arithmetical ability but also your understanding of the calculations when placed in 'real life' situations. These could involve percentages, ratios, fractions or decimals – or a combination of two or more of these.

Tackle these by restating to yourself exactly what you are being asked, that is put the problem into its simplest terms, perhaps writing it down for yourself as a sum.

Question

The initial price of two dresses was £50 each but they were both reduced to half price in a sale. The following week they were both reduced by a further 10%. They then both sold to the same person. How much did she pay in total?

Answer

£45.00

Explanation

You should understand that this question is asking you to solve a calculation that, in its simplest terms, would read £50 ÷ 2 – 10% × 2 = ? Work out the final price of each dress by first dividing by two to get the half price figure, then deducting a further 10%. Finally, multiply by two because, remember, there were two dresses bought.

Calculation: £50.00 ÷ 2 = £25.00 minus 10% (£2.50) = £22.50 × 2 = £45.00

NUMBER SEQUENCES

Here you must find the number that completes a sequence of numbers. If you are practised in using numbers, finding the solution can become almost automatic. The answer is obvious and you may not think about how you found it. If, however, you are not so familiar with using numbers, there are ways to tackle these questions to make them easier. We have all learned to count – forwards and backwards – at a very early age and counting is just a basic number sequence. From being a difficult and almost incomprehensible process in our very early childhood, counting becomes something that, by the time we reach the end of our schooldays, we do automatically.

However, you will obviously encounter more difficult number sequences if they form part of your tests and you need to know how to tackle them. The first step is to work out the difference between each pair of numbers in the sequence. Jot it down. You are looking for a pattern. Try this example, which again includes multiple choices for the answer:

Question

Find the next number in the series 7, 9, 8, 10, 9, 11, ?

a 9   **b** 12   **c** 7   **d** 8   **e** 10

Answer

e 10 is correct.

Explanation

If you jotted down the differences between each pair of numbers, you should have spotted the pattern $+2, -1, +2, -1, +2$ so you need to subtract 1 from 11 to get the final number in the sequence and get the correct answer 10.

2 TESTS BASED ON TABLES, GRAPHS AND CHARTS

The next two timed tests examine your ability to locate and use information given in graphs and charts of different kinds. These could include the most common types like the column chart shown as an example here or pie charts with which everyone is familiar or more unusual ones such as doughnut charts (like pie charts but doughnut shaped!) or scatter diagrams (charts with the data points scattered on the graph). Whichever type is used, your task will be the same – to find the relevant information quickly and accurately and use it to answer the questions.

You will find that you are allowed more time for this type of question. This is because the individual questions are more complicated. You are not presented with a simple calculation as in the arithmetic section but have to decide for yourself exactly what information you need to find to solve the problem and then look for it in the chart or graph. This may involve several separate calculations using the information. It is important that you continue to work methodically and accurately. Although you are allowed more time for each question, you will nevertheless need to work as quickly as possible. There will be no time to waste.

A TABLE

Use Table 1.1 to answer the following questions.

Table 1.1 Production, deliveries and reject product statistics

Year	Quarter	Total Production 000s Tonnes	Paper Delivered 000s Tonnes	Paper Rejected 000s Tonnes
2006	1st	100	91.9	8.1
	2nd	95	92.0	3.0
	3rd	100	87.6	12.4
	4th	78	71.2	8.8
2005	1st	90	88.0	2.0
	2nd	80	75.0	5.0
	3rd	95	94.1	0.9
	4th	80	77.0	3.0
2004	1st	80	65.0	15.0
	2nd	60	55.0	5.0
	3rd	80	78.0	2.0
	4th	60	58.0	20

1 How many more tonnes of paper were produced in 2006 than in 2004?

a 345,000

b 28

c 18,000

d 28,000

e 93,000

2 How does paper production in 2004 compare with 2005?

a Increased by 12.3%

b Decreased by 2.3%

c Increased by 6.5%

d Increased by 18.8%

e Increased by 23.2%

3 Approximately what percentage of total production was rejected in the first quarter of 2004?

a 10

b 18.75

c 8

d 12.5

e 20.3

4 What approximate percentage of paper produced in 2006 was delivered?

a 92

b 98

c 8

d 3.73

Answers

1 **e** 93,000

2 **e** Increased by 23.2%

3 **b** 18.75%

4 **a** 92%

Explanations

1 Answer **e** 93,000 is correct. Add up separate totals for total production for 2006 and for 2004 then subtract the 2004 total from the total for 2006, i.e. 373 − 280 = 93. Do not forget that the paper production is expressed in 000s tonnes.

2 Answer **e** Increased by 23.2% is correct. Calculate the total production for each of the two years in question. Find the difference between these two year's production totals. Divide by the lower figure (because there is an increase from 2004 to 2005) then multiply by 100 to find the percentage increase.

3 Answer **b** 18.75% is correct. To find the rejected amount as a percentage of the total produced, divide 15.0 (rejected in Q1 2004) by 80 (total produced in Q1 2004) then express as a percentage by multiplying by 100.

Recall the formula for % change:

$$\% \text{ change} = \frac{\text{actual change}}{\text{original whole}} \times 100\%$$

4 Answer **a** 92% is correct. Express the delivered quantity as a percentage of the total, i.e. 342.7 ÷ 373 × 100 = 91.88 = approx 92%.

A COLUMN CHART

As this is a sample question and you are not working against any time limits here, take a good look at the chart before

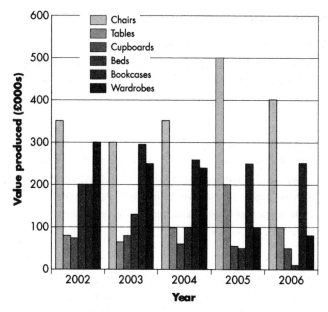

Figure 1.1 Column chart – furniture production figures 2002–06

attempting the questions below. Pay particular attention to the information given around the chart.

Use the information given in Figure 1.1 to answer the following questions:

1 What was the greatest percentage fall in chair production from one year to the next?

a 14.3%

b 20%

c 25%

d 43%

e 70%

2 In what year did bookcase production represent two thirds of wardrobe production?

a 2002

b 2003

c 2004

d 2005

e 2006

3 In the highest producing year overall, approximately what proportion of total production did chairs represent?

a 29%

b 5%

c 89%

d 15%

e 90%

4 In the year that bed production was 66% of wardrobe production, what was the value of chair and table production combined?

a £360,000

b £500,000

c £430,000

d £400,000

e £350,000

Answers

1 **b** 20%

2 **e** 2006

3 **a** 11%

4 **c** £430,000

Explanations

1 Answer **b** 20% is correct. Only two of the years show a
   year-on-year fall in chair production – 2003 and 2006. The
   greater of these is 2006, i.e. from 500 to 400. Express the
   difference as a percentage by dividing the difference by
   the production figure for 2005 (the original whole) and
   multiply by 100 (100 ÷ 500 × 100 = 20).

2 Answer **a** 2002 is correct. The easiest way to tackle this
   question is to look for the most likely year then to check
   the calculation. For example, the year 2005 can be
   eliminated straight away as bookcase production
   exceeds wardrobe production so it is obviously not two
   thirds. You are looking for something slightly more than
   half. When you think that the year 2002 looks about
   right, check by calculating the difference in fraction
   terms (300 × 2/3 = 200).

3 Answer **a** 29% is correct. Work out a total production
   value for each year by adding together the totals of the
   six types of furniture within each year. 2002 is the highest
   producing year overall with £1205 (000s). In that year
   £350 (000s) chairs were produced. You can see at a
   glance that this is approximately a third or calculate to
   check (350 ÷ 1205 × 100 = 29.04%).

4 Answer **c** £430,000 is correct. 66% is two-thirds so look first for the year where bed production is two-thirds of wardrobe production. That is 2002 when beds were 200 and wardrobes were 300. Then read off the value of chairs (350) and tables (80), add them together remembering that the answer should be given in £000s.

3 Quantitative relations tests – these are useful practice for the UK Civil Service Fast Stream Qualifying Tests

These two timed tests serve two purposes – firstly, they provide tests for general use. The questions are centred on algebra and the section of explanations for these tests will start with a brief overview of the basics of algebra for all the people – and there are an enormous number – who haven't consciously encountered any algebra since they left school and are scared of tackling it now. These questions testing your understanding of basic algebraic principles may be scattered throughout other numerical tests or they may be grouped together and used when the employer deems that the deductive thought processes demonstrated by mastery of these questions is of particular importance to the job area in question. Secondly, tests of this type form an important part of the UK Civil Service Fast Stream Qualifying Tests for graduate entry into the Civil Service. Completing plenty of practice on these tests will help you a great deal if this is your aim. You must get through the Qualifying Tests if you are to go on to the group assessment centre – the Civil Service Selection Board. This includes more written tests, group exercises and interviews.

In this sort of test, paying attention to the instructions as to how you must indicate your answer is of particular importance. Usually – especially for the Civil Service tests – you will be asked to mark your answers by shading in a box with a pencil. This is because an Optical Mark Reader is used to score the tests so it essential that your answers are clear enough and in a form that the machine can interpret. The machine will ignore ticks and crosses or marks that are too light and your answer will be marked as wrong automatically. Don't forget that any rough work should not be carried out on the test paper in this case – your jottings could be mistaken for your answers!

Just one more warning on this type of test – take extra care that you are putting the answer to each question in the appropriate space. It is surprisingly easy to work quickly through your answers, getting all your answers right but, because you have not noticed that you have not lined up your answers correctly, you will not get any points at all.

Take a look at these instructions and then attempt the sample question:

INSTRUCTIONS

Three or four numbers are laid out in a row and four or five rows make up each question. Your task is to identify the numerical relationship in the first three or four rows and then to apply that same relationship to the final row to find the missing number.

You must indicate your answer by shading in the appropriate boxes as shown in this example:

Sample Question

A	B	C
5	3	7
6	4	8
9	3	15
11	7	15
7	4	?

The answer to this example is 10 and you should indicate your answer as shown in the first of these three boxes – the remaining two boxes show you how NOT to indicate your answer.

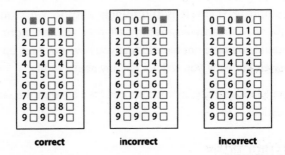

correct   incorrect   incorrect

The explanation for working out this example is as follows:

Formula = 2a − b = c

(2 × 7) − 4 = ?

Therefore ? = 10

If you have difficulties understanding this example then turn quickly to the short discussion of basic algebra in the explanations section, which should help you, or consult a basic mathematics book. Now that you have seen how the questions are formulated and how to answer them, try this one:

Question

What is the relationship between the rows of numbers? Use algebraic formulae to find the missing figure (?) in the final row.

A	B	C	
			0 □ 0 □ 0 □
			1 □ 1 □ 1 □
			2 □ 2 □ 2 □
3	2	5	3 □ 3 □ 3 □
			4 □ 4 □ 4 □
5	4	7	5 □ 5 □ 5 □
9	5	17	6 □ 6 □ 6 □
			7 □ 7 □ 7 □
12	11	14	8 □ 8 □ 8 □
12	?	10	9 □ 9 □ 9 □

Answer

The answer is 13

Explanations

Formula = $3a - 2b = c$

$(3 \times 12) - (2 \times ?) = 10$

Therefore $? = 13$

Remember to indicate your answer as 0 hundreds, 1 ten and 3 units.

PROBLEMS AND PITFALLS

Now that we have seen how the questions, answers and explanations will be laid out in later chapters, we can look at the problems and pitfalls associated with numerical tests in general.

For example, it is absolutely essential that you read the instructions carefully. Ask yourself a few questions as you read:

- What exactly are you being asked to do?
- How should you indicate your answers?
- Are you allowed to use a calculator?
- Can you write on the question paper?
- Or has some spare paper been supplied for the purpose of rough calculations?
- Do you need to estimate the answer?

These are general things that you should look out for but there are also some pitfalls that are associated with specific types of questions. You will find many of these highlighted in this book when the individual questions are explained – see Chapter 3. Here are a few guidelines for avoiding some of the problems and pitfalls you may come across:

- With tests where you have to write your answers on a separate sheet of paper check from time to time that you are writing your answers in the right place. It is easy – especially if you have to miss out a difficult question or are working under time constraints – to continue down the answer sheet totally unaware that your answers are wrong simply because they are written in the wrong space.

- If you come across figures enclosed in brackets, always try to solve the sum inside the brackets before going on to the rest of the question. For example: 6 + (9 × 5) = ? Work out 9 × 5 = 45 first, then add 6 = 51.

- Don't panic if you come across a negative number. Remember that −1 is still a number so it would still be a valid answer.

- A negative multiplied by a negative is always a positive (e.g. −2 × −2 = +4).

- A negative number multiplied by a positive number is always a negative (e.g. −2 × 3 = −6).

- With number sequences you must work systematically. Work out the difference between the first and second numbers, then the second and third and so on. Consider the four arithmetical operations (add, subtract, multiply and divide) in turn.

- If you're working with graphs and charts, pay particular attention to details contained around the diagram. You must read and note the details given in the key to a diagram. If a figure for steel production of 10 is given, ask yourself '10 what?' – 10 tonnes, 10,000 tonnes? The answer to this question will be in the key.

NOW TRY THE TESTS

Hopefully you are now convinced that preparation, including testing yourself using the tests in this book, will definitely improve your performance – and your chances of getting that job or promotion. So, on with the tests. . .

CHAPTER TWO
TIMED TESTS

Having looked at the variety of tests that you may be asked to take at this level, we now come to the most important part of this book – the timed tests. Work through these quickly but as accurately as possible, noting your answers and keeping a careful eye on the time allowed for each test.

Try to make your practice sessions as close to a real test as possible. For instance, work in a quiet area where you are unlikely to be disturbed, only use your calculator where it is indicated that you may do so, record your answers in an organised way and use plenty of extra paper to do your rough calculations. When using your calculator, it is customary to give your answers correct to only two decimal places.

GENERAL MATHEMATICAL

TEST 1

(Answers to this test can be found on pages 117–125.)

Allow yourself 28 minutes for this test.

Answer the following questions without using a calculator.

1 1934 + 24,555 − 18 = ?

2 (16 × 3) ÷ 8 = ?

3 −12 + 8 = ?

4 4 − 5 − 2 = ?

5 3 + 15 − (6 × 2) = ?

6 150 × 6 = ?

7 (288 − 16) × 3 = ?

8 1060 + 25 − 5 = ?

9 (99 ÷ 3) − 16 = ?

10 (28 × 3) ÷ 12 = ?

You may use a calculator to answer the remainder of the questions in this test.

11 $\frac{3}{4} + \frac{2}{3} = ?$

12 $2\frac{1}{4} \div 3 = ?$

13 $\frac{1}{2} \div 4 = ?$

14 2.3 + 5.78 = ?

15 7 − 1.6 = ?

16 $0.33 + 1.5 + 6 = ?$

17 $1.5 \times 45 = ?$

18 45% of 3000 = ?

19 5% of 25,500 = ?

20 £10 + 17.5% = ?

For the remainder of this test you must choose from the selection of five answers, only one of which is correct.

21 One thousand books were put on sale at a cover price of £7.99. Half sold at this price but 250 were sold at a 25% discount, 100 at 10% discount and the remainder were unsold. How much money was taken in total?

  a £6212.22

  b £5493.12

  c £719.10

  d £1498.12

  e £6121.22

22 If a maintenance contract costs £87 per month and a technician call-out when not under a maintenance contract is priced at £325, how many call-outs per year would make the contract worthwhile?

  a 4

  b 5

  c 6

  d 7

  e 8

23 If every 250 bottles of bleach require 16.25 litres of solvent to produce, how much solvent is required to produce 6500 bottles of bleach?

a 42.3 litres

b 100.0 litres

c 121.9 litres

d 422.5 litres

e 1219.0 litres

24 Last year's sales target was £265,000. This year's is £328,000. By what percentage has this year's sales target increased over last year's?

a 17%

b 29%

c 43%

d 81%

e None of these

25 A total of 5200 analyses last month required 17,300 hours of computer time. Approximately how much computer time would be required to perform an additional 300 analyses if all other factors remain unchanged?

a 330 hours

b 540 hours

c 660 hours

d 940 hours

e 1000 hours

26 A batch of shampoo requires 510 litres of herbal extracts and 13,400 litres of water. What is the approximate ratio of water to herbal extracts?

a 26:1

b 3.8:1

c 1:26

d 1:38

e 1:260

27 Temporary staff are paid £6.00 per hour. If 47 hours were worked last week by each of 7 temporary staff, what was the total bill?

a £197

b £282

c £329

d £846

e £1974

28 If 625 kg of fruit are required to produce 200 jars of jam, approximately how much fruit is required to produce 450 jars of jam?

a 144 kg

b 531 kg

c 864 kg

d 1270 kg

e 1406 kg

29 A survey carried out on 1500 people showed that 37% liked a new product, while 32% were indifferent. If the rest said they disliked the product, how many people were in this category?

a 48

b 237

c 465

d 945

e 1020

30 In an average week, the computer is down for 2.75 hours. Lost revenue per hour is £425,000. What is the approximate total revenue (to 2 decimal places) lost in a 52-week year?

a £0.23m

b £8.04m

c £12.10m

d £47.26m

e £60.78m

For the next ten questions in this test, you must find the missing number in the sequence (indicated by ?). There is a selection of five answers, only one of which is correct.

31 29, 30, 32, 35, 39, ?

  a 41

  b 42

  c 46

  d 45

  e 44

32 45, 67, 89, 101, 112, ?

  a 63

  b 131

  c 123

  d 132

  e 109

33 155, 165, 170, 180, 185, ?

  a 195

  b 200

  c 190

  d 205

  e 210

34 70, 80, 160, 170, 340, ?

  a 350

  b 360

  c 370

  d 380

  e 400

35 512, 256, 128, 64, 32, ?

  a 30

  b 20

  c 16

  d 8

  e 4

36 81, 87, 84, 90, 87, ?

  a 90

  b 93

  c 96

  d 84

  e 81

37 1, 3, 3, 9, 27, ?

  a 48

  b 36

  c 243

  d 241

  e 263

38 2, −4, 6, −8, 10, ?

  a −14

  b 14

  c −10

  d −12

  e 12

39 16, 17, 19, 22, 26, ?

  a 27

  b 28

  c 29

  d 30

  e 31

40 1, 8, 27, 64, 125, ?

a 244

b 216

c 198

d 224

e 220

TEST 2

(Answers to this test can be found on pages 126–131.)

You may use a calculator to answer the following questions. Allow yourself 29 minutes.

1 1234 + 29 − 137 = ?

2 66 ÷ 4 = ?

3 (900 ÷ 3) × 2 = ?

4 (49 ÷ 7) × 8 = ?

5 (19 × 1000) + 16,754 = ?

6 (63 ÷ 9) − 2 = ?

7 (9 × 7) + 484 = ?

8 (903 + 17) × 3 = ?

9 (21 + 67) ÷ 11 = ?

10 100,666 × 3 = ?

For the next ten questions in this test, you must estimate the answers. Note the word ESTIMATE. For each question you are required to choose the answer, from the five answers given, which is nearest to your estimate.

11 24.1 × 0.85 = ?

a 16

b 220

c 19

d 24

e 20

12 76% of 15,605 = ?

  a 11,880

  b 11,860

  c 11,940

  d 12,000

  e 10,180

13 $\frac{1}{5}$ of 297 = ?

  a 34

  b 59

  c 70

  d 54

  e 66

14 How many minutes in two days?

  a 6000

  b 5600

  c 6400

  d 4400

  e 2880

15 Estimate the number of words in a book of 210 pages with an average of 250 words per page.

  a 59,000

  b 58,000

  c 20,000

  d 52,500

  e 57,000

16 $401 - 903 = ?$

  a 1300

  b 500

  c −500

  d −400

  e −1300

17 50% of 9389 = ?

  a 3700

  b 3900

  c 4200

  d 4700

  e 5000

18 £2529.83 + £1447.21 = ?

a £3975

b £3973

c £3980

d £3929

e £9385

19 89% of 635 = ?

a 700

b 565

c 520

d 510

e 500

20 $\frac{3}{16}$ of £50 = ?

a £6.75

b £9.50

c £15.25

d £6.20

e £6.00

The next ten questions in this test are word problems based on percentages, decimals and fractions. You may use a calculator.

21 A company's operating profit last year was £7.75 million. If there is an increase this year of 13%, what will this year's operating profit be?

 a £7,945,000

 b £8,126,800

 c £8,346,200

 d £8,757,500

 e None of these

22 Of a total of 225 employees, 32% are female. 89% of female employees are between the ages of 20 and 35. How many employees are females between the ages of 20 and 35?

 a 12

 b 58

 c 64

 d 89

 e 201

23 If a department makes a profit of 30% on a turnover of £85,000, what percentage profit can be expected if overheads increase by £10,000 but other factors remain unchanged?

  a 5%

  b 10%

  c 14%

  d 18%

  e 25%

24 A basic working week is 37.5 hours for which the hourly-pay rate is £6.50. Overtime after this is paid at 'time and a half' for the first four hours and 'double time' for the remainder. How much would you earn if you worked 45 hours?

  a £243.75

  b £358.25

  c £328.25

  d £325.25

  e £292.50

25 A computer costs £1250, a scanner £99 and a printer £145 (all excluding VAT). With VAT added at 17.5%, what would be the total cost?

a £1655.99

b £1694.45

c £1494.00

d £1755.45

e £1800.00

26 A new car costs £15,000. Each year it decreases in value by 25% of the value at the start of that year. What is its value after 3 years?

a £4000.00

b £3750.00

c £6328.13

d £7300.15

e £6500.00

27 A shop sells computer games at £20. If the cost price is £12, what is the percentage profit?

a 33%

b 67%

c 40%

d 60%

e 45%

28 What would be the total selling price of a suit with a cost price of £75 plus a shirt with a cost price of £17.50 if both were sold at a profit of 40%?

a £149.50

b £92.50

c £175.00

d £129.50

e £105.00

29 How many millimetres are there in 3.2 inches. 1 inch = 25.4 mm.

a 81.28

b 76.2

c 82

d 72

e 80.3

30 Two pies are divided between five children. The first two get one-third of a pie each, the third child gets a half and the fourth a quarter. How much is left for the fifth child?

a $\frac{5}{12}$

b $\frac{7}{12}$

c $\frac{1}{3}$

d $\frac{1}{4}$

e $\frac{1}{2}$

For the final ten questions in this test you are required to find the missing number in the sequence (indicated by ?). There is a selection of five answers, only one of which is correct.

31 10, 15, 22.5, 33.75, 50.63, ?

  a 83

  b 75.10

  c 75.94

  d 65.5

  e 95.94

32 20, 16, 12.8, 10.24, 8.19, ?

  a 6.55

  b 5.55

  c 7.55

  d 6.17

  e 5.97

33 11, 30, 49, 68, ?, 106

  a 85

  b 86

  c 87

  d 88

  e 89

34 83, 166, 332, ?, 1328, 2656

  a 974

  b 1128

  c 964

  d 900

  e 664

35 84, 91, 98, 105, 112, ?

  a 118

  b 119

  c 120

  d 121

  e 122

36 840, 827, 814, 801, 788, ?

  a 772

  b 773

  c 774

  d 775

  e 762

37 4, 12, 36, 108, ?, 972

  a 424

  b 324

  c 285

  d 365

  e 522

38 390,625, 78,125, 15,625, 3125, 625, ?

  a 125

  b 150

  c 550

  d 500

  e 250

39 8, 11, 19, 30, 49, ?

  a 60

  b 69

  c 59

  d 79

  e 128

40 34, 567, 8910, 1112, 1314, ?

   a 1516

   b 1506

   c 1485

   d 1617

   e 1819

TESTS BASED ON TABLES, GRAPHS AND CHARTS

TEST 3

(Answers to this test can be found on pages 131–138.)

Using the data shown in the relevant table, chart or graph as indicated, answer the following questions, allowing yourself 34 minutes. You may use a calculator.

Use the data in Tables 2.1 and 2.2 to solve the following ten questions.

Table 2.1 UK sales figures

Representative	Number of orders	Value of orders (£000s)	Average order value (£000s)	Salary (£p.a.)
John	24	216	?	21,600
Sue	40	200	5	21,000
Pete	6	126	?	19,500
Sally	10	100	10	20,000
Jim	15	135	9	20,000

Table 2.2 Export sales figures

Representative	Number of orders	Value of orders (€000s)	Average order value (€000s)	Salary (£p.a.)
Colin	29	400	13.8	41,000
Bill	50	310	6.2	40,000
Ian	13	387.5	?	30,000

1 Using an exchange rate of £:euro of 1:1.55, what was the highest average order value attained by any representative?

a £21,000

b £19,230

c £29,800

d £21

e £12,970

2 What is the average order value of each of the salesperson's average sales? NB Use an exchange rate of £:euro of 1:1.55.

a £12,970

b £19,250

c £10,766

d £12,000

e £29,800

3 What was the ratio of order value to salary of the second highest earner?

a 1:6.29

b 1:7.75

c 1:5

d 1:40

e 1:310

4 What is the difference between the highest and the lowest average order values?

a £23,600

b £16

c £15,000

d £17

e £17,000

5 By what percentage was the highest export salary greater than the lowest UK salary?

a 110%

b 5%

c 95%

d 25%

e 47%

6 By how much does the average order value of the top earner in the UK exceed that of the second highest earner in the UK?

a £9000

b £4

c £4000

d £5000

e £600

7 By what percentage does the average export salary exceed the average UK salary?

a 16%

b 19%

c 75%

d 78%

e 81%

8 Express the ratio of the average number of orders per UK sales person to the average number of orders per export sales person in its simplest form.

a 1:3

b 95:92

c 92:57

d 57:92

e 31:19

9 Omitting the top two UK representatives, what was the value of UK orders?

a £777,000

b £361,000

c £36,100

d £3610

e £361

10 The target for export orders was 1 million euros. By what percentage did the result exceed this?

   a 9.75%

   b 9%

   c 7%

   d 1%

   e 10%

Use the pie charts shown in Figures 2.1 and 2.2 to answer the following five questions.

Function

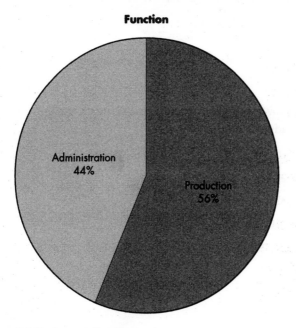

Administration 44%

Production 56%

Figure 2.1 Pie chart – staff profiles, year 1

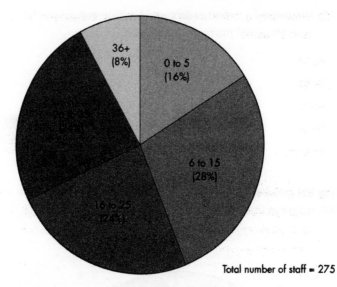

Figure 2.2 Pie chart – length of service of administrative and production staff (in years)

11 How many more production staff are there than administrative staff?

a 12

b 27

c 33

d 110

e Cannot tell

12 How many administrative staff have served between 10 and 20 years?

  a 31

  b 57

  c 72

  d 89

  e Cannot say

13 How many administrative staff are there in the 26 to 35 years' service group, if the proportion of production staff and administration staff is the same for this group as for the overall group?

  a 11

  b 29

  c 37

  d 49

  e 52

14 If half of the 0 to 5 years' service group and all of the 36+ years' service group are production staff, how many production staff are there altogether in the other groups?

  a 110

  b 132

  c 164

  d 231

  e Cannot tell

15 If 50% of the production staff plus 12 members of staff from the administrative department were to leave the company, how many members of staff would be left in total?

a 89

b 98

c 186

d 275

e 77

Using the data shown in Table 2.3 and the column chart in Figure 2.3, answer the following five questions.

Table 2.3 Sales figures – years 1 to 3 (£000s)

Product group	Year1	Year 2	Year 3
A	1,420	1,560	1,610
B	2,670	2,940	2,880
C	4,100	3,690	3,140
D	2,360	2,830	3,120
E	930	1,040	860

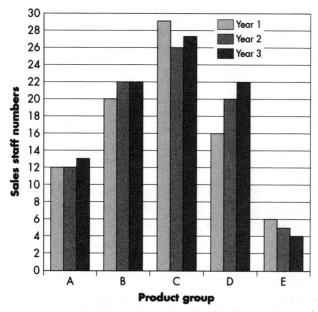

Figure 2.3 Sales department – staff numbers, years 1 to 3

16 By what percentage did total sales staff numbers change from Year 1 to Year 3?

  a 2.3%

  b 3.5%

  c 4.8%

  d 6.0%

  e 9.4%

17 Which product group achieved the best sales results per sales person in Year 2?

a Product group A

b Product group B

c Product group C

d Product group D

e Product group E

18 Which product group's sales figures for Years 1 to 3 show the closest trend to its sales staff numbers over the same period?

a Product group A

b Product group B

c Product group C

d Product group D

e Product group E

19 If there are 7 additional sales staff in Year 3, and the average sales per person remains constant, how much greater would the total sales for Year 3 be?

a £12,500

b £855,500

c £923,500

d £1,253,400

e Cannot say

20 In the year that the sales of product group E were at their lowest, what was the average amount of this product group sold per sales person?

a £930,000

b £115,600

c £215,000

d £860,000

e £1,040,000

Using the details contained in Figure 2.4, answer the remaining questions in this test.

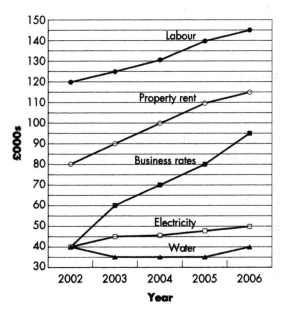

Figure 2.4 Operating costs

21 What was the total cost over five years of the highest cost item of expenditure?

a £670,000

b £14,500

c £66,100

d £661,000

e £145,000

22 What percentage of total expenditure in 2002 was the amount spent on property rent in that year?

a 15%

b 20%

c 30%

d 25%

e 50%

23 What was the percentage increase in the amount spent on business rates from 2002 to 2006?

a 137.5%

b 95%

c 105%

d 37.5%

e 110%

24 How much more, over the five-year period, was spent on electricity than on water?

  a £229,000

  b £185,000

  c £4400

  d £40,000

  e £44,000

25 How much less in total was spent in 2002 than in 2006?

  a £125,000

  b £320,000

  c £445,000

  d £225,000

  e £115,000

TEST 4

(Answers to this test can be found on pages 138–143.)

Use the data contained in the tables, charts and graphs as indicated to answer the questions in this test. You may use a calculator. Allow yourself 40 minutes.

Use the data contained in Table 2.4 to answer the next ten questions.

Table 2.4 Train timetable – Chesterford to Middletown

	Chesterford	Whitebank	Neartown	Longdale	Middletown
Mon–Fri	06.40	07.00	07.45	08.20	08.30
	09.45	10.05	10.50	11.25	11.35
	15.30	15.50	16.35	17.10	17.20
	20.45	21.05	21.50	22.25	22.35
Saturday	07.30	07.45	08.30	09.00	09.10
	08.15	08.30	09.15	09.45	09.55
	09.30	09.45	10.30	11.00	11.10
	14.00	14.15	15.00	15.30	15.40
Sunday	10.30	11.00	12.00	12.40	12.55
	15.50	16.20	17.20	18.00	18.15

NB: All train journeys are the same duration on the same day and return journeys take the same time as the outward journey over the same route on the same day.

1 How much longer would it take to get from Chesterford to Longdale travelling on Sunday than if you did the same journey on Monday?

   a 1 hour

   b 30 minutes

   c 45 minutes

   d 1 hour 30 minutes

   e 35 minutes

2 How long would a journey from Chesterford to Middletown take on Tuesday if there was a delay of 20 minutes at Neartown?

   a 1 hour 30 minutes

   b 1 hour 40 minutes

   c 1 hour 50 minutes

   d 2 hours 10 minutes

   e 2 hours

3 If a further train was provided to run on Sunday to leave Chesterford at 12.30, what time would it be scheduled to arrive in Middletown?

   a 14.30

   b 13.50

   c 13.55

   d 14.50

   e 14.55

4 A man travelled from Whitebank to Longdale on Saturday and returned on Sunday. What was his total travelling time?

a 2 hours 50 minutes

b 2 hours 55 minutes

c 3 hours

d 3 hours 5 minutes

e 3 hours 10 minutes

5 A train driver operates two return journeys from Chesterford to Middletown on each day from Monday to Thursday and one return journey on Sunday. How many hours does he work in total, assuming that the return journeys take the same amount of time as the outward journeys?

a 27 hours 45 minutes

b 29 hours 50 minutes

c 34 hours 10 minutes

d 33 hours 30 minutes

e 35 hours

6 What would be the total travelling time of a return journey between Whitebank and Middletown on Sunday?

a 3 hours 30 minutes

b 3 hours 40 minutes

c 3 hours 50 minutes

d 4 hours

e 4 hours 10 minutes

7 How much longer does it take to travel from Chesterford to Middletown on Sunday than it takes to travel from Longdale to Middletown on Monday?

a 2 hours 25 minutes

b 2 hours 15 minutes

c 2 hours 35 minutes

d 1 hour 45 minutes

e 1 hour 25 minutes

8 If Saturday's last train is delayed by a fault on the line and arrives at Neartown one hour and ten minutes late, what time will it be scheduled to arrive in Middletown?

a 15.00

b 16.10

c 17.00

d 16.50

e 16.40

9 The train due to leave Chesterford at 08.15 on Saturday is cancelled and the 09.30 departure is brought forward by 15 minutes. What time would this train now arrive at Whitebank?

a 09.15

b 09.30

c 09.45

d 10.00

e 10.15

10 A man makes the outward journey from Whitebank to Neartown by train from Monday to Friday each week and also takes an extra journey from Whitebank to Middletown on Saturdays. How much time will he have spent on trains after four weeks?

a 15 hours

b 5 hours 10 minutes

c 20 hours 40 minutes

d 21 hours 40 minutes

e 15 hours 40 minutes

Using the pie chart in Figure 2.5, answer the next ten questions.

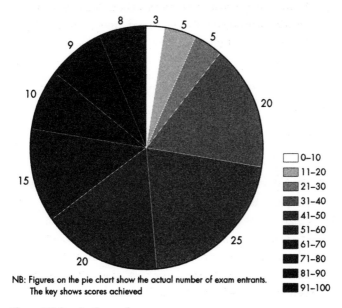

NB: Figures on the pie chart show the actual number of exam entrants.
The key shows scores achieved

Figure 2.5 Examination marks

11 How many people in total entered the examination?

   a 130

   b 140

   c 125

   d 100

   e 120

12 Approximately what percentage of entrants were in the largest score group?

   a 30%

   b 40%

   c 25%

   d 21%

   e 50%

13 If the pass mark for this examination was 55%, how many people in total passed?

   a 80

   b 45

   c 20

   d 78

   e Cannot tell

14 All entrants who obtained scores between 21 and 50 were offered the chance to re-sit the examination and 40% of these were successful. How many passed at the re-sit?

   a 20

   b 25

   c 50

   d 45

   e Cannot tell

15 Approximately what percentage of the total number of entrants obtained marks in the very top score bracket?

a 10

b 8

c 20

d 7

e 100

16 How many more people obtained scores of 51% or over than obtained scores of 50% or less?

a 50

b 58

c 4

d 62

e 6

17 Approximately what percentage of entrants obtained scores of 51% or more?

a 60

b 40

c 62

d 52

e 42

18 If the pass mark for this examination was 51%, how many people in total failed?

a 58

b 62

c 51

d 50

e 60

19 How many more people obtained scores in the top 10% than scored 10% or less?

a 8

b 3

c 5

d 10

e 0

20 What percentage of entrants obtained scores of between 41% and 70%?

a 25%

b 45%

c 50%

d 60%

e 65%

Use the column chart in Figure 2.6 to answer the following ten questions.

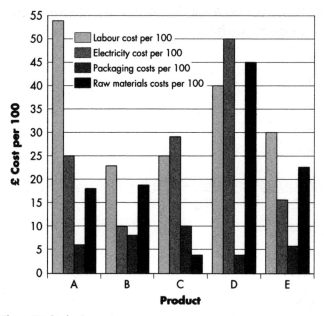

Figure 2.6 Production costs

21 If labour costs were excluded, what would be the production costs per 100 of product A?

a £103

b £101

c £49

d £51

e £25

22 How much would labour costs be in total for 100 of each
of the five products?

a £172

b £103

c £54

d £127

e £142

23 If a customer ordered 200 each of products A and E, how
much would the raw material costs for that order be?

a £82

b £109

c £218

d £36

e £41

24 What is the total cost per 100 of the most expensive
product to produce?

a £119

b £54

c £139

d £172

e £103

25 Which is the least expensive product to produce?

a Product A

b Product B

c Product C

d Product D

e Product E

26 What is the difference, in £ per 100, between the labour costs of the most expensive product to produce (taking into account all four types of cost shown) and the least expensive?

a £139

b £17

c £80

d £60

e £79

27 If the manufacturing company produces 500 of each product in a week, what would be their labour costs for four weeks?

a £760

b £1780

c £2225

d £3440

e £688

28 Labour costs are the greatest cost area that the manufacturers have to meet. How much do they spend at the second highest cost area to produce 100 of each of the five products?

a £172

b £130

c £109

d £445

e £139

29 The company develops a new product and the raw material costs of this product are 15% higher than the average raw material costs of the existing 5 products. What would be the approximate raw material costs per 100 of this new product?

a £25

b £104

c £105

d £89

e £99

30 If the company achieves its target in the coming year to reduce overall production costs of product B by 10%, what would be the new total production cost per 100 of this product?

a £60

b £45

c £66

d £54

e £109

Using the information shown in Figure 2.7, solve the final ten problems in this test.

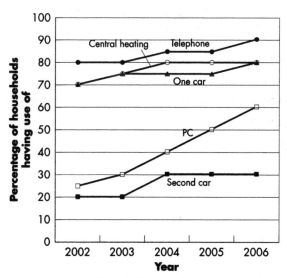

Number of households surveyed 1000.

Figure 2.7 Household survey

31 By what percentage did the access to telephones increase between 2003 and 2006?

   a 5%

   b 10%

   c 80%

   d 90%

   e 85%

32 How many more of the households surveyed had use of a second car in 2006 than in 2004?

   a 30%

   b 300

   c 0

   d 100

   e Cannot say

33 Which item showed the greatest change in ownership during the period shown?

   a PC

   b Telephone

   c Central heating

   d One car

   e Second car

34 How many more households had use of a telephone in 2006 than in 2005?

a 500

b 850

c 5%

d 50

e 900

35 If 50 more households have the use of a second car in 2007, what percentage of the households surveyed would then have access to a second car?

a 40%

b 25%

c 30%

d 350

e 35%

36 How many more households owned a PC in 2006 compared with 2002?

a 400

b 350

c 300

d 250

e 200

37 If all the households that have use of a PC in 2006 also had a telephone, how many people had a telephone but not a PC?

a 400

b 200

c 900

d 600

e 300

38 Which two items showed the lowest increase in percentage of households having use of them between 2002 and 2005?

a PC and telephone

b Central heating and second car

c One car and a second car

d Telephone and one car

e PC and central heating

39 How many households had both central heating and the use of two cars in 2005?

a 300

b 800

c 500

d 0

e Cannot tell

40 In 2002 how many more households had use of the item
with the largest percentage compared with the item with
the lowest percentage?

a 300

b 400

c 500

d 600

e 700

QUANTITATIVE RELATIONS

The next eight timed tests require you to identify the numerical relationship between A, B and C in each of the first four rows in the following questions and use it to work out the value of the missing number (indicated by ?) in the fifth row. The relationship uses the same algebraic formula in each row.

Indicate your answer in the grid provided. Full instructions on how to use this method of showing your answer are given in Chapter 1. Allow yourself 10 minutes for each test.

TEST 5

(Answers to this test can be found on pages 145–146.)

1

A	B	C
2	3	5
7	8	15
4	2	6
19	2	21
8	23	?

```
0☐ 0☐ 0☐
1☐ 1☐ 1☐
2☐ 2☐ 2☐
3☐ 3☐ 3☐
4☐ 4☐ 4☐
5☐ 5☐ 5☐
6☐ 6☐ 6☐
7☐ 7☐ 7☐
8☐ 8☐ 8☐
9☐ 9☐ 9☐
```

2

A	B	C
8	3	5
14	3	11
7	1	6
9	3	6
?	8	16

```
0☐ 0☐ 0☐
1☐ 1☐ 1☐
2☐ 2☐ 2☐
3☐ 3☐ 3☐
4☐ 4☐ 4☐
5☐ 5☐ 5☐
6☐ 6☐ 6☐
7☐ 7☐ 7☐
8☐ 8☐ 8☐
9☐ 9☐ 9☐
```

3

A	B	C
5	4	11
2	1	5
8	6	18
9	22	5
5	?	3

```
0□0□0□
1□1□1□
2□2□2□
3□3□3□
4□4□4□
5□5□5□
6□6□6□
7□7□7□
8□8□8□
9□9□9□
```

4

A	B	C
8	2	3
15	3	6
4	2	1
21	3	9
?	2	4

```
0□0□0□
1□1□1□
2□2□2□
3□3□3□
4□4□4□
5□5□5□
6□6□6□
7□7□7□
8□8□8□
9□9□9□
```

5

A	B	C
27	3	9
14	2	7
16	2	8
18	6	3
21	3	?

```
0□0□0□
1□1□1□
2□2□2□
3□3□3□
4□4□4□
5□5□5□
6□6□6□
7□7□7□
8□8□8□
9□9□9□
```

6

A	B	C
6	9	2
4	4	3
20	6	10
15	9	5
8	6	?

```
0□0□0□
1□1□1□
2□2□2□
3□3□3□
4□4□4□
5□5□5□
6□6□6□
7□7□7□
8□8□8□
9□9□9□
```

7

A	B	C
5	3	7
8	4	12
19	8	30
14	2	26
7	?	10

0 ☐	0 ☐	0 ☐
1 ☐	1 ☐	1 ☐
2 ☐	2 ☐	2 ☐
3 ☐	3 ☐	3 ☐
4 ☐	4 ☐	4 ☐
5 ☐	5 ☐	5 ☐
6 ☐	6 ☐	6 ☐
7 ☐	7 ☐	7 ☐
8 ☐	8 ☐	8 ☐
9 ☐	9 ☐	9 ☐

8

A	B	C
6	3	12
18	2	22
8	9	26
45	3	51
?	5	21

0 ☐	0 ☐	0 ☐
1 ☐	1 ☐	1 ☐
2 ☐	2 ☐	2 ☐
3 ☐	3 ☐	3 ☐
4 ☐	4 ☐	4 ☐
5 ☐	5 ☐	5 ☐
6 ☐	6 ☐	6 ☐
7 ☐	7 ☐	7 ☐
8 ☐	8 ☐	8 ☐
9 ☐	9 ☐	9 ☐

TEST 6

(Answers to this test can be found on pages 146–148.)

1

A	B	C
3	15	6
4	8	2
8	16	4
20	48	14
6	?	7

```
0☐ 0☐ 0☐
1☐ 1☐ 1☐
2☐ 2☐ 2☐
3☐ 3☐ 3☐
4☐ 4☐ 4☐
5☐ 5☐ 5☐
6☐ 6☐ 6☐
7☐ 7☐ 7☐
8☐ 8☐ 8☐
9☐ 9☐ 9☐
```

2

A	B	C
6	6	72
5	3	30
12	4	96
8	3	48
14	2	?

```
0☐ 0☐ 0☐
1☐ 1☐ 1☐
2☐ 2☐ 2☐
3☐ 3☐ 3☐
4☐ 4☐ 4☐
5☐ 5☐ 5☐
6☐ 6☐ 6☐
7☐ 7☐ 7☐
8☐ 8☐ 8☐
9☐ 9☐ 9☐
```

3

A	B	C
5	3	11
9	2	13
45	8	61
3	25	53
18	6	?

```
0☐ 0☐ 0☐
1☐ 1☐ 1☐
2☐ 2☐ 2☐
3☐ 3☐ 3☐
4☐ 4☐ 4☐
5☐ 5☐ 5☐
6☐ 6☐ 6☐
7☐ 7☐ 7☐
8☐ 8☐ 8☐
9☐ 9☐ 9☐
```

4

A	B	C
14	7	7
6	1	5
93	89	4
16	4	12
?	3	29

```
0☐ 0☐ 0☐
1☐ 1☐ 1☐
2☐ 2☐ 2☐
3☐ 3☐ 3☐
4☐ 4☐ 4☐
5☐ 5☐ 5☐
6☐ 6☐ 6☐
7☐ 7☐ 7☐
8☐ 8☐ 8☐
9☐ 9☐ 9☐
```

5

A	B	C
10	3	17
6	3	9
20	6	34
4	1	7
9	?	1

```
0☐ 0☐ 0☐
1☐ 1☐ 1☐
2☐ 2☐ 2☐
3☐ 3☐ 3☐
4☐ 4☐ 4☐
5☐ 5☐ 5☐
6☐ 6☐ 6☐
7☐ 7☐ 7☐
8☐ 8☐ 8☐
9☐ 9☐ 9☐
```

6

A	B	C
2	8	3
5	13	4
6	20	7
7	21	7
5	95	?

```
0☐ 0☐ 0☐
1☐ 1☐ 1☐
2☐ 2☐ 2☐
3☐ 3☐ 3☐
4☐ 4☐ 4☐
5☐ 5☐ 5☐
6☐ 6☐ 6☐
7☐ 7☐ 7☐
8☐ 8☐ 8☐
9☐ 9☐ 9☐
```

7

A	B	C
5	4	40
3	3	18
10	6	120
9	5	90
4	?	16

```
0 □ 0 □ 0 □
1 □ 1 □ 1 □
2 □ 2 □ 2 □
3 □ 3 □ 3 □
4 □ 4 □ 4 □
5 □ 5 □ 5 □
6 □ 6 □ 6 □
7 □ 7 □ 7 □
8 □ 8 □ 8 □
9 □ 9 □ 9 □
```

8

A	B	C
18	3	6
21	3	7
90	10	9
25	5	5
?	8	2

```
0 □ 0 □ 0 □
1 □ 1 □ 1 □
2 □ 2 □ 2 □
3 □ 3 □ 3 □
4 □ 4 □ 4 □
5 □ 5 □ 5 □
6 □ 6 □ 6 □
7 □ 7 □ 7 □
8 □ 8 □ 8 □
9 □ 9 □ 9 □
```

TEST 7

(Answers to this test can be found on pages 148–149.)

1

A	B	C
14	2	6
18	12	3
42	32	5
23	5	9
36	4	?

```
0☐ 0☐ 0☐
1☐ 1☐ 1☐
2☐ 2☐ 2☐
3☐ 3☐ 3☐
4☐ 4☐ 4☐
5☐ 5☐ 5☐
6☐ 6☐ 6☐
7☐ 7☐ 7☐
8☐ 8☐ 8☐
9☐ 9☐ 9☐
```

2

A	B	C
6	4	3
20	5	8
10	5	4
9	3	6
25	?	5

```
0☐ 0☐ 0☐
1☐ 1☐ 1☐
2☐ 2☐ 2☐
3☐ 3☐ 3☐
4☐ 4☐ 4☐
5☐ 5☐ 5☐
6☐ 6☐ 6☐
7☐ 7☐ 7☐
8☐ 8☐ 8☐
9☐ 9☐ 9☐
```

3

A	B	C
1	16	5
18	24	2
4	22	6
3	24	7
6	27	?

```
0☐ 0☐ 0☐
1☐ 1☐ 1☐
2☐ 2☐ 2☐
3☐ 3☐ 3☐
4☐ 4☐ 4☐
5☐ 5☐ 5☐
6☐ 6☐ 6☐
7☐ 7☐ 7☐
8☐ 8☐ 8☐
9☐ 9☐ 9☐
```

4

A	B	C
5	4	13
11	3	17
7	10	27
6	5	16
8	?	20

```
0☐ 0☐ 0☐
1☐ 1☐ 1☐
2☐ 2☐ 2☐
3☐ 3☐ 3☐
4☐ 4☐ 4☐
5☐ 5☐ 5☐
6☐ 6☐ 6☐
7☐ 7☐ 7☐
8☐ 8☐ 8☐
9☐ 9☐ 9☐
```

5

A	B	C
4	3	11
14	2	30
9	7	25
6	45	57
18	?	39

```
0☐ 0☐ 0☐
1☐ 1☐ 1☐
2☐ 2☐ 2☐
3☐ 3☐ 3☐
4☐ 4☐ 4☐
5☐ 5☐ 5☐
6☐ 6☐ 6☐
7☐ 7☐ 7☐
8☐ 8☐ 8☐
9☐ 9☐ 9☐
```

6

A	B	C
6	2	14
3	2	8
7	5	19
2	1	5
?	7	21

```
0☐ 0☐ 0☐
1☐ 1☐ 1☐
2☐ 2☐ 2☐
3☐ 3☐ 3☐
4☐ 4☐ 4☐
5☐ 5☐ 5☐
6☐ 6☐ 6☐
7☐ 7☐ 7☐
8☐ 8☐ 8☐
9☐ 9☐ 9☐
```

7

A	B	C
5	3	30
5	4	40
2	7	28
6	2	24
3	3	?

0 ☐	0 ☐	0 ☐
1 ☐	1 ☐	1 ☐
2 ☐	2 ☐	2 ☐
3 ☐	3 ☐	3 ☐
4 ☐	4 ☐	4 ☐
5 ☐	5 ☐	5 ☐
6 ☐	6 ☐	6 ☐
7 ☐	7 ☐	7 ☐
8 ☐	8 ☐	8 ☐
9 ☐	9 ☐	9 ☐

8

A	B	C
5	3	18
2	3	9
2	9	27
1	2	4
?	4	16

0 ☐	0 ☐	0 ☐
1 ☐	1 ☐	1 ☐
2 ☐	2 ☐	2 ☐
3 ☐	3 ☐	3 ☐
4 ☐	4 ☐	4 ☐
5 ☐	5 ☐	5 ☐
6 ☐	6 ☐	6 ☐
7 ☐	7 ☐	7 ☐
8 ☐	8 ☐	8 ☐
9 ☐	9 ☐	9 ☐

TEST 8

(Answers to this test can be found on pages 149–150.)

1

A	B	C
8	3	3
25	12	7
14	3	6
7	4	2
9	2	?

```
0□ 0□ 0□
1□ 1□ 1□
2□ 2□ 2□
3□ 3□ 3□
4□ 4□ 4□
5□ 5□ 5□
6□ 6□ 6□
7□ 7□ 7□
8□ 8□ 8□
9□ 9□ 9□
```

2

A	B	C
16	5	26
5	8	21
3	20	43
6	17	40
5	?	23

```
0□ 0□ 0□
1□ 1□ 1□
2□ 2□ 2□
3□ 3□ 3□
4□ 4□ 4□
5□ 5□ 5□
6□ 6□ 6□
7□ 7□ 7□
8□ 8□ 8□
9□ 9□ 9□
```

3

A	B	C
4	8	19
17	3	22
6	7	19
3	23	48
?	9	25

```
0□ 0□ 0□
1□ 1□ 1□
2□ 2□ 2□
3□ 3□ 3□
4□ 4□ 4□
5□ 5□ 5□
6□ 6□ 6□
7□ 7□ 7□
8□ 8□ 8□
9□ 9□ 9□
```

4

A	B	C
14	2	7
21	7	3
45	9	5
81	9	9
?	14	2

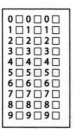

5

A	B	C
14	2	6
14	6	4
27	3	12
14	8	3
34	18	?

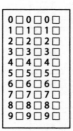

6

A	B	C
4	2	12
5	4	18
1	3	8
5	8	26
?	4	24

7

A	B	C
5	3	7
1	5	8
2	8	13
4	14	23
6	4	?

```
0□ 0□ 0□
1□ 1□ 1□
2□ 2□ 2□
3□ 3□ 3□
4□ 4□ 4□
5□ 5□ 5□
6□ 6□ 6□
7□ 7□ 7□
8□ 8□ 8□
9□ 9□ 9□
```

8

A	B	C
29	8	7
5	3	0
21	5	6
49	15	10
?	8	5

```
0□ 0□ 0□
1□ 1□ 1□
2□ 2□ 2□
3□ 3□ 3□
4□ 4□ 4□
5□ 5□ 5□
6□ 6□ 6□
7□ 7□ 7□
8□ 8□ 8□
9□ 9□ 9□
```

TEST 9

(Answers to this test can be found on pages 150–151.)

1

A	B	C
14	4	5
19	3	8
5	1	2
8	2	3
11	3	?

```
0☐ 0☐ 0☐
1☐ 1☐ 1☐
2☐ 2☐ 2☐
3☐ 3☐ 3☐
4☐ 4☐ 4☐
5☐ 5☐ 5☐
6☐ 6☐ 6☐
7☐ 7☐ 7☐
8☐ 8☐ 8☐
9☐ 9☐ 9☐
```

2

A	B	C
5	2	2
23	12	6
17	2	8
11	6	3
8	?	3

```
0☐ 0☐ 0☐
1☐ 1☐ 1☐
2☐ 2☐ 2☐
3☐ 3☐ 3☐
4☐ 4☐ 4☐
5☐ 5☐ 5☐
6☐ 6☐ 6☐
7☐ 7☐ 7☐
8☐ 8☐ 8☐
9☐ 9☐ 9☐
```

3

A	B	C
24	3	8
9	3	3
18	6	3
81	9	9
?	2	7

```
0☐ 0☐ 0☐
1☐ 1☐ 1☐
2☐ 2☐ 2☐
3☐ 3☐ 3☐
4☐ 4☐ 4☐
5☐ 5☐ 5☐
6☐ 6☐ 6☐
7☐ 7☐ 7☐
8☐ 8☐ 8☐
9☐ 9☐ 9☐
```

4

A	B	C
5	23	9
1	7	3
4	18	7
3	19	8
9	?	45

```
0 □ 0 □ 0 □
1 □ 1 □ 1 □
2 □ 2 □ 2 □
3 □ 3 □ 3 □
4 □ 4 □ 4 □
5 □ 5 □ 5 □
6 □ 6 □ 6 □
7 □ 7 □ 7 □
8 □ 8 □ 8 □
9 □ 9 □ 9 □
```

5

A	B	C
7	4	15
23	7	37
3	14	31
8	9	26
?	8	30

```
0 □ 0 □ 0 □
1 □ 1 □ 1 □
2 □ 2 □ 2 □
3 □ 3 □ 3 □
4 □ 4 □ 4 □
5 □ 5 □ 5 □
6 □ 6 □ 6 □
7 □ 7 □ 7 □
8 □ 8 □ 8 □
9 □ 9 □ 9 □
```

6

A	B	C
5	3	18
7	8	64
2	3	9
2	10	30
?	3	21

```
0 □ 0 □ 0 □
1 □ 1 □ 1 □
2 □ 2 □ 2 □
3 □ 3 □ 3 □
4 □ 4 □ 4 □
5 □ 5 □ 5 □
6 □ 6 □ 6 □
7 □ 7 □ 7 □
8 □ 8 □ 8 □
9 □ 9 □ 9 □
```

7

A	B	C
2	10	4
7	25	9
24	36	6
35	45	5
8	?	3

```
0 □ 0 □ 0 □
1 □ 1 □ 1 □
2 □ 2 □ 2 □
3 □ 3 □ 3 □
4 □ 4 □ 4 □
5 □ 5 □ 5 □
6 □ 6 □ 6 □
7 □ 7 □ 7 □
8 □ 8 □ 8 □
9 □ 9 □ 9 □
```

8

A	B	C
3	3	2
5	3	6
15	19	10
8	4	11
11	6	?

```
0 □ 0 □ 0 □
1 □ 1 □ 1 □
2 □ 2 □ 2 □
3 □ 3 □ 3 □
4 □ 4 □ 4 □
5 □ 5 □ 5 □
6 □ 6 □ 6 □
7 □ 7 □ 7 □
8 □ 8 □ 8 □
9 □ 9 □ 9 □
```

TEST 10

(Answers to this test can be found on pages 151–152.)

1

A	B	C
4	6	6
7	2	19
9	6	21
5	1	14
10	?	27

```
0☐ 0☐ 0☐
1☐ 1☐ 1☐
2☐ 2☐ 2☐
3☐ 3☐ 3☐
4☐ 4☐ 4☐
5☐ 5☐ 5☐
6☐ 6☐ 6☐
7☐ 7☐ 7☐
8☐ 8☐ 8☐
9☐ 9☐ 9☐
```

2

A	B	C
95	3	98
4	7	11
18	18	36
5	21	26
?	16	20

```
0☐ 0☐ 0☐
1☐ 1☐ 1☐
2☐ 2☐ 2☐
3☐ 3☐ 3☐
4☐ 4☐ 4☐
5☐ 5☐ 5☐
6☐ 6☐ 6☐
7☐ 7☐ 7☐
8☐ 8☐ 8☐
9☐ 9☐ 9☐
```

3

A	B	C
7	3	8
4	4	8
9	5	12
2	6	10
1	7	?

```
0☐ 0☐ 0☐
1☐ 1☐ 1☐
2☐ 2☐ 2☐
3☐ 3☐ 3☐
4☐ 4☐ 4☐
5☐ 5☐ 5☐
6☐ 6☐ 6☐
7☐ 7☐ 7☐
8☐ 8☐ 8☐
9☐ 9☐ 9☐
```

4

A	B	C
21	3	9
17	1	8
9	5	2
10	2	4
65	?	2

```
0 □ 0 □ 0 □
1 □ 1 □ 1 □
2 □ 2 □ 2 □
3 □ 3 □ 3 □
4 □ 4 □ 4 □
5 □ 5 □ 5 □
6 □ 6 □ 6 □
7 □ 7 □ 7 □
8 □ 8 □ 8 □
9 □ 9 □ 9 □
```

5

A	B	C
2	5	15
6	3	21
5	2	12
4	9	45
4	8	?

```
0 □ 0 □ 0 □
1 □ 1 □ 1 □
2 □ 2 □ 2 □
3 □ 3 □ 3 □
4 □ 4 □ 4 □
5 □ 5 □ 5 □
6 □ 6 □ 6 □
7 □ 7 □ 7 □
8 □ 8 □ 8 □
9 □ 9 □ 9 □
```

6

A	B	C
9	3	3
12	4	3
21	7	3
30	10	3
?	8	3

```
0 □ 0 □ 0 □
1 □ 1 □ 1 □
2 □ 2 □ 2 □
3 □ 3 □ 3 □
4 □ 4 □ 4 □
5 □ 5 □ 5 □
6 □ 6 □ 6 □
7 □ 7 □ 7 □
8 □ 8 □ 8 □
9 □ 9 □ 9 □
```

7

A	B	C
5	2	11
17	6	39
8	11	26
9	17	34
?	3	14

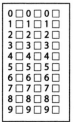

8

A	B	C
14	27	1
7	3	11
30	10	50
3	1	5
19	?	36

TEST 11

(Answers to this test can be found on pages 152–153.)

1

A	B	C
5	3	30
8	9	144
20	2	80
12	6	144
10	5	?

```
0☐ 0☐ 0☐
1☐ 1☐ 1☐
2☐ 2☐ 2☐
3☐ 3☐ 3☐
4☐ 4☐ 4☐
5☐ 5☐ 5☐
6☐ 6☐ 6☐
7☐ 7☐ 7☐
8☐ 8☐ 8☐
9☐ 9☐ 9☐
```

2

A	B	C
3	2	3
8	4	11
30	25	34
4	5	2
?	3	14

```
0☐ 0☐ 0☐
1☐ 1☐ 1☐
2☐ 2☐ 2☐
3☐ 3☐ 3☐
4☐ 4☐ 4☐
5☐ 5☐ 5☐
6☐ 6☐ 6☐
7☐ 7☐ 7☐
8☐ 8☐ 8☐
9☐ 9☐ 9☐
```

3

A	B	C
5	6	16
11	5	20
52	3	57
7	7	20
?	9	30

```
0☐ 0☐ 0☐
1☐ 1☐ 1☐
2☐ 2☐ 2☐
3☐ 3☐ 3☐
4☐ 4☐ 4☐
5☐ 5☐ 5☐
6☐ 6☐ 6☐
7☐ 7☐ 7☐
8☐ 8☐ 8☐
9☐ 9☐ 9☐
```

4

A	B	C
20	4	14
32	3	19
12	2	8
8	14	18
16	2	?

0 □	0 □	0 □	
1 □	1 □	1 □	
2 □	2 □	2 □	
3 □	3 □	3 □	
4 □	4 □	4 □	
5 □	5 □	5 □	
6 □	6 □	6 □	
7 □	7 □	7 □	
8 □	8 □	8 □	
9 □	9 □	9 □	

5

A	B	C
8	2	3
21	3	9
14	10	2
19	3	8
9	?	3

0 □	0 □	0 □	
1 □	1 □	1 □	
2 □	2 □	2 □	
3 □	3 □	3 □	
4 □	4 □	4 □	
5 □	5 □	5 □	
6 □	6 □	6 □	
7 □	7 □	7 □	
8 □	8 □	8 □	
9 □	9 □	9 □	

6

A	B	C
5	9	6
20	57	3
10	1	29
7	19	2
8	4	?

0 □	0 □	0 □	
1 □	1 □	1 □	
2 □	2 □	2 □	
3 □	3 □	3 □	
4 □	4 □	4 □	
5 □	5 □	5 □	
6 □	6 □	6 □	
7 □	7 □	7 □	
8 □	8 □	8 □	
9 □	9 □	9 □	

7

A	B	C
6	5	16
18	9	36
11	5	21
3	20	43
?	15	36

```
0□ 0□ 0□
1□ 1□ 1□
2□ 2□ 2□
3□ 3□ 3□
4□ 4□ 4□
5□ 5□ 5□
6□ 6□ 6□
7□ 7□ 7□
8□ 8□ 8□
9□ 9□ 9□
```

8

A	B	C
6	4	9
8	12	22
5	5	10
2	6	10
?	9	15

```
0□ 0□ 0□
1□ 1□ 1□
2□ 2□ 2□
3□ 3□ 3□
4□ 4□ 4□
5□ 5□ 5□
6□ 6□ 6□
7□ 7□ 7□
8□ 8□ 8□
9□ 9□ 9□
```

TEST 12

(Answers to this test can be found on pages 153–154.)

1

A	B	C
6	3	21
5	10	60
6	7	49
4	9	45
3	?	20

```
0 □ 0 □ 0 □
1 □ 1 □ 1 □
2 □ 2 □ 2 □
3 □ 3 □ 3 □
4 □ 4 □ 4 □
5 □ 5 □ 5 □
6 □ 6 □ 6 □
7 □ 7 □ 7 □
8 □ 8 □ 8 □
9 □ 9 □ 9 □
```

2

A	B	C
14	4	36
19	3	44
4	24	56
5	6	22
100	?	208

```
0 □ 0 □ 0 □
1 □ 1 □ 1 □
2 □ 2 □ 2 □
3 □ 3 □ 3 □
4 □ 4 □ 4 □
5 □ 5 □ 5 □
6 □ 6 □ 6 □
7 □ 7 □ 7 □
8 □ 8 □ 8 □
9 □ 9 □ 9 □
```

3

A	B	C
11	2	5
9	2	4
18	3	8
60	3	29
14	7	?

```
0 □ 0 □ 0 □
1 □ 1 □ 1 □
2 □ 2 □ 2 □
3 □ 3 □ 3 □
4 □ 4 □ 4 □
5 □ 5 □ 5 □
6 □ 6 □ 6 □
7 □ 7 □ 7 □
8 □ 8 □ 8 □
9 □ 9 □ 9 □
```

4

A	B	C
5	7	1
4	5	2
7	9	3
13	15	9
8	10	?

```
0□ 0□ 0□
1□ 1□ 1□
2□ 2□ 2□
3□ 3□ 3□
4□ 4□ 4□
5□ 5□ 5□
6□ 6□ 6□
7□ 7□ 7□
8□ 8□ 8□
9□ 9□ 9□
```

5

A	B	C
4	16	6
3	19	8
7	21	7
36	40	2
2	?	3

```
0□ 0□ 0□
1□ 1□ 1□
2□ 2□ 2□
3□ 3□ 3□
4□ 4□ 4□
5□ 5□ 5□
6□ 6□ 6□
7□ 7□ 7□
8□ 8□ 8□
9□ 9□ 9□
```

6

A	B	C
5	3	3
11	4	8
43	4	40
15	7	9
7	3	?

```
0□ 0□ 0□
1□ 1□ 1□
2□ 2□ 2□
3□ 3□ 3□
4□ 4□ 4□
5□ 5□ 5□
6□ 6□ 6□
7□ 7□ 7□
8□ 8□ 8□
9□ 9□ 9□
```

7

A	B	C
20	3	7
14	3	4
10	4	1
12	3	3
?	5	8

```
0 □ 0 □ 0 □
1 □ 1 □ 1 □
2 □ 2 □ 2 □
3 □ 3 □ 3 □
4 □ 4 □ 4 □
5 □ 5 □ 5 □
6 □ 6 □ 6 □
7 □ 7 □ 7 □
8 □ 8 □ 8 □
9 □ 9 □ 9 □
```

8

A	B	C
40	5	85
15	3	33
6	1	13
9	18	36
7	23	?

```
0 □ 0 □ 0 □
1 □ 1 □ 1 □
2 □ 2 □ 2 □
3 □ 3 □ 3 □
4 □ 4 □ 4 □
5 □ 5 □ 5 □
6 □ 6 □ 6 □
7 □ 7 □ 7 □
8 □ 8 □ 8 □
9 □ 9 □ 9 □
```

TEST 13

Finally, here's a test that contains a mixture of the various types of questions.

(Answers to this test can be found on pages 154–157.)

Allow yourself 15 minutes.

Answer the following questions without using a calculator.

1 $477 + 29.2 + (14.4 \times 2) - 33 = ?$

2 $((23 \times 7) - 1) \div 8 = ?$

3 $(546 - 269) \times 76 = ?$

For the next three questions in this test, you must estimate the answers. Note the word ESTIMATE. For each question you are required to choose the answer, from the five answers given, which is nearest to your estimate.

4 $1650 \div 29 = ?$

a 16

b 220

c 57

d 34

e 70

5 $2.5 \times 29.6 = ?$

a 75

b 12

c 45

d 85

e 100

6 $(\frac{1}{2} + 49.4) \times 1000 = ?$

a 63300

b 500

c 4990

d 24400

e 49900

The next three questions in this test are word problems based on percentages, decimals and fractions. You may use a calculator.

7 A business calculated its profits at £575,655 but, due to an oversight, further costs of £23,246 for wages and a ten per cent increase in property rent had to be deducted from this. If the property rent was originally £18,500, what would the correct profit figure be?

a £550,560

b £617,401

c £533,909

d £550,559

e None of these

8 A company has calculated that 15% of its male employees have a degree, while only 5% of its female employees have a similar qualification. If it employs 120 women and 40 men, how many in total have degrees?

a 21

b 11

c 12

d 5

e 6

9 If a charity has an income of £7,005,558 in the current year and plans to increase this in the coming year by a sixth, how much will the income be next year?

a £9,173,151

b £6,789,511

c £8,731,511

d £8,173,151

e None of these

For the next three questions in this test you are required to find the missing number in the sequence (indicated by ?). There is a selection of five answers, only one of which is correct.

10 100, 75, 56.25, 42.19, 31.64, 23.73, ?

  a 18

  b 19.3

  c 17.8

  d 25.2

  e None of these

11 49, 53, 55, 59, 61, 65, ?

  a 67

  b 69

  c 71

  d 57

  e 73

12 95.3, 93.5, 94.5, 92.7, 93.7, 91.9, ?

  a 95.3

  b 89.1

  c 90.1

  d 93.9

  e 92.9

Using the data shown in the following charts, answer the next five questions. You may use a calculator.

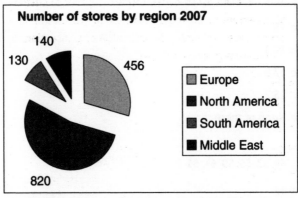

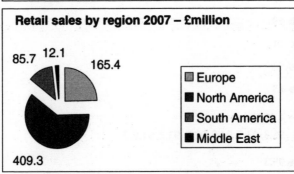

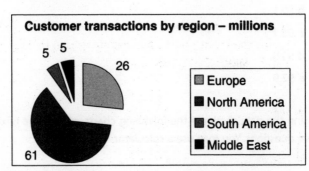

Figure 2.8 Pie charts – number of stores, retail sales and customer transactions by region

13 By how many transactions did the number of customer transactions in the region with the largest number of stores exceed the number of customer transactions in all the other regions combined?

a 25

b 94

c 25 million

d 25

e 35 million

14 What was the total value of retail sales for the entire store group?

a £692.5

b £672.5

c £409.3 million

d £672 million

e £672.5 million

15 By how many stores does the total of stores in North and South America exceed the number of stores in Europe and the Middle East combined?

a 354

b 364

c 345

d 596

e 950

16 What was the average number of transactions per store in the Middle East in 2007?

a 35147

b 85653

c 74390

d 37541

e 35714

17 What was the average sales value per store throughout the entire group in 2007?

a £435,000

b £4,350,000

c £43 million

d £53 million

e £5.3 million

The final two questions in this test require you to identify the numerical relationship between A, B and C in each of the first four rows and use it to work out the value of the missing number (indicated by ?) in the fifth row. The relationship uses the same algebraical formula in each row.

Indicate your answer in the grid provided.

18

A	B	C
55	8	16
29	12	6
85.5	26.5	20
12.5	1.5	4
93	67	?

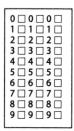

19

A	B	C
21	2	84
45	1	90
9	3	54
4	8	64
18	5	?

CHAPTER THREE
ANSWERS TO AND EXPLANATIONS OF TIMED TESTS

GENERAL MATHEMATICAL

TEST 1

This uncomplicated section is a mixture of questions testing your knowledge of the four basic rules of arithmetic – addition, subtraction, multiplication and division. It is this type of question where practice should really help you. Getting plenty of practice on this type of question will improve your accuracy and also increase the speed with which you work. These are basic numerical skills, so improving your performance in this section will also help with other types of numerical test.

If you find that you are struggling with the basic arithmetic sections, ask yourself whether it is because of the time constraints or because you have difficulty using the four basic rules. If you feel that the problem is that you are too tense or that you panic because you are working against the clock, go to Chapter 4. Look at the relaxation techniques and advice, then put some into practice. If, however, you think that you need a better understanding of arithmetic, get some help. Go back to basics by finding a course – enquire at your local college for this. Alternatively, you could buy yourself a good basic maths book. You might also benefit from some individual tuition in basic arithmetic.

Unless you have got all of this section correct, you would benefit from more practice and also from a little revision of the basic concepts. Some suggestions include:

- Know your multiplication tables
- Try to visualise the addition and subtraction problems. If you can picture putting the figures to be added together one under the other – just as you would do if you were writing the sum down on paper – it might help to avoid mistakes and you might see the solution a little quicker
- Remember to work out the figures inside a pair of brackets first, then continue with the calculation
- Practise, practise, practise!

Questions of this type will usually be straightforward and not have any particular traps or pitfalls. However, certain areas frequently cause difficulty for many people so extra explanation is included where appropriate with the answers below:

1 The answer is 26,471.

2 The answer is 6. Always work out the calculation in the brackets first.

3 The answer is −4. Negative numbers are still numbers – learn the basic principles and they will become as easy for you to deal with as positive numbers, with which we are all more familiar. Some people find that negative numbers become more comprehensible if they imagine a scale in

the form of a line with 0 in the middle and positive numbers extending out to the right and negative numbers going out from the 0 to the left as shown below:

−10 −9 −8 −7 −6 −5 −4 −3 −2 −1 0 +1 +2 +3 +4 +5 +6 +7 +8 +9 +10

If you had any difficulty at all with questions 3 and 4 in this section, try doing them again using a scale like the one above.

4 The answer is −3.

5 The answer is 6.

6 The answer is 900.

7 The answer is 816.

8 The answer is 1080.

9 The answer is 17.

10 The answer is 7.

Calculations involving percentages and fractions can cause panic in many people – especially under test conditions and time constraints. However, it must be remembered that we use percentages and fractions every day. We are all familiar with interest rates shown in newspapers and fractions used in shops – the offer of half price goods or 'a third off' for example.

What we sometimes fail to appreciate is that percentages and fractions are closely connected. Percentages are, in fact, fractions expressed as parts of one hundred. This helps us with comparison of increases or decreases by using a common standard – the one part in a hundred method, i.e. 1 per cent of a quantity is one-hundredth of it.

Fraction calculations are usually best tackled by converting to improper fractions by finding the common denominator (the number at the bottom of the fraction into which all the denominators in the question can be divided).

With this in mind, we can look at the questions in this next section.

11 The answer is $1\frac{5}{12}$. With denominators of 3 and 4, it is easy to see that the common denominator, which will enable you to work out your answer to this question, is 12. You can then state the question as $\frac{9}{12} + \frac{8}{12} = \frac{17}{12} = 1\frac{5}{12}$.

12 The answer is $\frac{3}{4}$. To solve this problem convert the fraction to $\frac{9}{4}$ so that you can divide it by $\frac{3}{1}$. Dividing the number of quarters by three quickly gives you your answer of $\frac{3}{4}$.

13 The answer is $\frac{1}{8}$. To divide the fraction by four you need to multiply the denominator by four.

14 The answer is 8.08. This is a simple addition involving decimals. If you find this slightly confusing – especially under the pressure of time – write it down on your rough paper so that the decimal points are aligned, then do the addition.

15 The answer is 5.4. A quick way to work this out in your head is to round up the 1.6 to 2 (so you have added 0.4) then subtract the 2 from 7 and add the 0.4 back on. With practice, this sort of operation will become so familiar that you may not even realise that that is what you are doing.

16 The answer is 7.83. Place these figures one under the other, not forgetting that 6 should be stated as 6.0 so that you can keep the decimal places aligned.

17 The answer is 67.5. Either work this out on paper, taking care about the decimal point, or alternatively, work it out in your head remembering that 1.5 is one and a half, i.e. add half of 45 on to 45.

18 The answer is 1350. The thought process for this calculation could be 45% of 100 is 45 so 45% of 1000 is 450. Multiply this by three to get the correct answer.

19 The answer is 1275. This is a similar calculation to that shown in question 8 above but an alternative way to show the calculation is $\frac{5}{100} \times 25,500$ (as 5% is five hundredths). Cancel that down so that you are left with 5×255 and you arrive at the correct answer of 1275.

20 The answer is £11.75. 17.5% of £1 is 17.5p so 17.5% of £10 is £1.75. Add this on to the original £10 to arrive at your answer.

Word problems at this level tend to be two-step calculations and therefore more difficult than at more basic levels. This means that you must take a more logical approach to them and, before you start working out the arithmetic, take a step back and ask yourself exactly what you are being asked. It often helps to restate the question in simple terms, discarding any extraneous details.

21 Answer **e** £6212.22 is correct. Calculate the different parts then add the three different figures together as follows:

500 @ £7.99	= £3995.00
250 @ £5.9925 (£7.99 − 25%)	= £1498.12
100 @ £7.191 (£7.99 − 10%)	= £719.10
Total	= £6212.22

22 Answer **a** 4 is correct. To answer this question you need to work out how many times more expensive the call-out fee is than the annual contract, but first you need to calculate the cost of the annual contract, i.e. 12 × 87 = 1044 then 1044 ÷ 325 = 3.21 = the breakeven point. This tells you that 3 call-outs would be less expensive than the annual contract whereas 4 call-outs would be more expensive.

23 Answer **d** 422.5 litres is correct. Here you must find out how many lots of 250 bottles are in the suggested production quantity of 6500 then multiply that by the quantity of solvent necessary to produce 250 bottles, i.e. 6500 ÷ 250 × 16.25.

24 Answer **e** None of these is correct. First of all work out the change from last year to this year = £63,000. You could try estimating what percentage increase this represents – it is a little less than a quarter or 25%. A glance at the choice of answers shows that none of them are around this figure so you could select the last option. Alternatively, you can use the percentage change formula to work it out precisely.

$$\% \text{ change} = \frac{\text{actual change}}{\text{original whole}} \times 100\%$$

25 Answer **e** 1000 hours is correct. Here is a good example of the value of restating the question simply. It asks you how long 300 analyses would take, so work out how long for each analysis then multiply by 300, i.e. 17,300 ÷ 5200 × 300 = 998. Note that the question asks 'approximately how much time' so the answer of 998 can be rounded up to 1000.

26 Answer **a** 26:1 is correct. In a ratio the numbers show the size of one quantity compared with the size of the other. It is important that they are always written in the same order as the quantities in the question, so in this example only the answers **a** or **b** are possible choices as the water is a larger quantity than the herbal extracts. If you cannot estimate the answer here, work it out by dividing 13,400 by 510.

27 Answer **e** £1974 is correct. This is a fairly straightforward question requiring you to calculate the number of hours worked in total then multiply by the hourly rate – simple to do with the help of your calculator.

28 Answer **e** 1406 kg is correct. There are two ways – at least – to solve this question. Firstly, you might see the relationship of 200 to 450 as 2.25 times. If this strikes you as you read the question, then continue and multiply 625 by 2.25 to get the answer. Alternatively, you could calculate as follows: $625 \div 200 \times 450 = 1406$.

29 Answer **c** 465 is correct. It is an advantage here to ask yourself 'what percentage disliked the product?' The answer to that is 31% so then you can work out 31% of 1500.

30 Answer **e** £60.78m is correct. This is easy with a calculator, i.e. $425 \times 2.75 \times 52$. As you can see, you can, in this case, discard the zeros as all the answers are sufficiently different but all given in millions.

To be successful with number sequence questions you must be able to spot the pattern in the numbers. As always, speed and accuracy are important. However, if you spend a little time now on your practice and on working through the explanations, you will soon see how the patterns develop and you will become quicker at completing this type of test. There are certain number sequences that come up time and time again and if you become familiar with these you may save yourself some time. Useful patterns in this respect include square roots (the square root of 16 is 4 for example), squared numbers (4 squared is 16, 3 squared is 9 and so on), basic multiplication tables and prime numbers (numbers that can only be divided by 1 and by themselves, i.e. 2, 3, 7, 11, 13 and so on).

Unless the pattern is immediately apparent to you, your first move when faced with a number sequence question should be to work out (and note down) the difference between each pair of figures. This will often give you the answer straight away if you can see a pattern in the differences you have noted down. Having tried the first set of number sequences in Chapter 2, work through the explanations given here.

31 Answer **e** 44 is correct. This is an easy sequence to start you off. Unless you immediately know the answer, write down the differences between each pair of digits and a well-known sequence will appear, i.e. 1, 2, 3, 4 and so on – a sequence we have all known for many years by the time we come to be applying for jobs and sitting these tests!

32 Answer **b** 131 is correct. Sometimes test compilers try to disguise a straightforward sequence as has been done here. It is simply counting up from 4 but the arrangement of the digits is designed to confuse.

33 Answer **a** 195 is correct. Again you should jot down the differences between each pair and look for a pattern. Here it is add 5, then add 10, then add 5, then 10 and so on.

34 Answer **a** 350 is correct. The pattern in this question is made more difficult to spot because it involves a combination of mathematical operations. If, as in this case, the numbers increase rapidly then it is likely that there is some element of multiplication. Bear this in mind and you should quickly spot the pattern of $+ 10$, $\times 2$, $+ 10$, $\times 2$ and so on.

35 Answer **c** 16 is correct. Here the numbers are halved each time. In contrast to the previous question, the number decreases rapidly so you should look for a pattern involving division.

36 Answer **b** 93 is correct. Look for the obvious patterns first. Here you should see that first 6 is added then 3 is subtracted and this pattern is repeated to the end of the sequence.

37 Answer **c** 243 is correct. This sequence is a common one. It involves multiplying the two previous digits. So $1 \times 3 = 3$, $3 \times 3 = 9$, $3 \times 9 = 27$ and so on.

38 Answer **d** −12 is correct. The positive and negative signs are added to this sequence to make the pattern more difficult to spot – they do not serve any other purpose than to confuse.

39 Answer **e** 31 is correct. Here there are two sequences in one. By jotting down the differences between each pair of numbers you will see the most common sequence of all – 1, 2, 3, 4, 5, 6 – being used to create another sequence.

40 Answer **b** 216 is correct. This is a very common sequence – the cubes of numbers.

TEST 2

If you get any of these first ten questions wrong, or find them difficult in any way, look back to Chapter 1 of this book and also to the first section in this chapter of explanations. The figures are slightly more difficult than the first section of arithmetic questions but, providing you work methodically and remember to work out the sum in the brackets before completing your calculation, they should not pose any real problems.

1 The answer is 1126.

2 The answer is 16.5.

3 The answer is 600.

4 The answer is 56.

5 The answer is 35,754.

6 The answer is 5.

7 The answer is 547.

8 The answer is 2760.

9 The answer is 8.

10 The answer is 301,998.

In this next section of ten questions you are being asked to estimate your answers and choose the answer nearest to the correct one. You will need to work quickly and will obviously not be allowed to use a calculator. In estimating, you need to develop the skill of rounding up or down as appropriate to make your calculation easier and quicker. Your estimating skills can be greatly improved with practice so do plenty of sums involving mental arithmetic and practise estimating your shopping bill as you go around the supermarket or play games involving scoring, such as darts or board games.

11 Answer **e** 20 is correct. This is an example of having to round up and down to facilitate calculations. 24.1 can be rounded down to 24 and 0.85 rounded up to 1. You will then know that the answer is less than 24.

12 Answer **b** 11,860 is correct. A very rough estimate of this answer could be obtained by rounding up 15,605 to 16,000. Three-quarters of this (75%) would be 12,000 so you know that this would be too much and this immediately eliminates two of the answers given. To get closer you could divide by 100 (to get 1%) by deleting the last two digits and then multiply by 76.

13 Answer **b** 59 is correct. Here you should round up 297 to 300 then divide by 5.

14 Answer **e** 2880 is correct. If you round up the number of hours in two days from 48 to 50 then multiply by minutes per hour, you would get 3000, which is slightly more than the correct answer so there is only one reasonable choice left to you.

15 Answer **d** 52,500 is correct. At 4 pages per 1000 words you could estimate that the total in 210 pages would be slightly more than 50,000 words.

16 Answer **c** −500 is correct. All the answers appear to have been rounded, so you know that the exact answer is not given, so ignore the units in both numbers in the question: 400 − 900 gives you −500. Remember that the number will be negative.

17 Answer **d** 4700 is correct. This is straightforward. Round up 9389 to 9400 and divide by 2 to get 50%.

18 Answer **c** £3980 is correct. A glance at the choice of answers tells you to ignore the pence in the question. Round up both amounts and add together to get your estimated answer.

19 Answer **b** 565 is correct. As 89% is so close to 90%, deduct (roughly) 10% from 635 to get 572 and then choose the closest answer.

20 Answer **b** £9.50 is correct. As $\frac{3}{16}$ is less than $\frac{1}{4}$, you know that the answer will be less than £12.50. Halve this again to get $\frac{1}{8}$ (or $\frac{2}{16}$). The answer is somewhere between these two figures. There is only one answer between £6.25 and £12.50.

21 Answer **d** £8,757,500 is correct. This simply requires you to increase £7.75 million by 13%. Ordinarily, this would mean that you would need to take care regarding the zeros on the end of the figure – a problem that causes many people to panic under test conditions – but in this case the answer choices make this unnecessary, proving that a quick glance at the answers in multiple-choice questions can often save you some time.

22 Answer **c** 64 is correct. Make sure that you read this question carefully. It is asking you to calculate 89% of 32% of 225 and the trap is that you will only calculate one or other of the percentages.

23 Answer **d** 18% is correct. Here you are being asked to work out what difference the increase in overheads makes to the profit percentage. The calculation is $(25.5 - 10) \div 85 \times 100 = $ percentage profit.

24 Answer **c** £328.25 is correct. There are three elements to the total pay – the basic pay (£243.75), the pay at 1.5 times the hourly rate (£39.00) and the pay at twice the standard rate (£45.50). You must split the hours into these three elements and then multiply by the appropriate hourly rate.

25 Answer **d** £1755.45 is correct. This is a straightforward question – add together the cost of the three items then add VAT at 17.5% to the total to get your answer.

26 Answer **c** £6328.13 is correct. The pitfall in this question is that you may simply deduct $3 \times 25\%$ from the cost of the new car. This would be incorrect as the question says that the depreciation of 25% is on 'the value at the start of that year' so the amount of decrease must change in line with the falling value of the car, i.e. £15,000 − 25%, then £11,250 − 25%, then £8,437.50 − 25% = £6328.13.

27 Answer **b** 67% is correct. The formula for calculating the percentage profit is

$$\text{percentage profit} = \frac{\text{price}}{\text{cost price}} \times 100$$

i.e. $\frac{8}{12} \times 100 = 67$

28 Answer **d** £129.50 is correct. As the profit margin is the same on both items, you can add the cost price of the suit and the shirt together then add 40% profit to your total to get the total price.

29 Answer **a** 81.28 is correct. A straightforward calculation using decimals, i.e. $3.2 \times 25.4 = 81.28$.

30 Answer **b** $\frac{7}{12}$ is correct. Once you have found the common denominator of 12, you will quickly see that $\frac{17}{12}$ have already been shared out and the remainder of the pies (two pies = $\frac{24}{12}$) will be $\frac{7}{12}$.

31 Answer **c** 75.94 is correct. This is a geometrical progression known as exponential growth. Each number is multiplied by 1.5. Note that they are rounded to two decimal places.

32 Answer **a** 6.55 is correct. This is another example of a geometrical progression but this time, with a decreasing sequence, it is known as exponential decay. The numbers are divided by 1.25 each time.

33 Answer **c** 87 is correct. This is a simple arithmetic progression where 19 is added between each pair of numbers.

34 Answer **e** 664 is correct. The numbers are doubled each time in this sequence. Where a sequence increases steeply like this you should look for an element of multiplication.

35 Answer **b** 119 is correct. Seven is added between each pair of numbers.

36 Answer **d** 775 is correct. Here you must subtract 13 each time to get the next number in the sequence.

37 Answer **b** 324 is correct. Here the numbers are multiplied by three each time.

38 Answer **a** 125 is correct. Here the sequence decreases dramatically so you should look for possible division. In this question, the numbers are divided by 5.

39 Answer **d** 79 is correct. You must add the two previous numbers together to get the next number in the sequence.

40 Answer **a** 1516 is correct. This sequence attempts to hide the most common sequence of all – simply counting upwards. Starting at 3 you should see that, although the digits are grouped in a different way it is simply a counting sequence from 3 to 16, i.e. if the commas were placed as we would expect to see them in this sequence, it would read 3, 4, 5, 6, 7, 8, 9, 10, 11 and so on.

TABLES, CHARTS AND GRAPHS

TEST 3

1 Answer **a** £21,000 is correct. First convert the three order values quoted in euros by dividing by the exchange rate then simply choose the highest value using both tables. NB Answer should be in £000s.

2 Answer **c** £10,766 is correct. First find all the missing pieces of information (in Table 2.1) and ensure that all values are converted to £ (in Table 2.2). Add all the average order values together and divide by 8 (the number of sales people) to find the average. Again, note that the answer is in £000s.

3 Answer **b** 1:7.75 is correct. First identify the second- highest earner (Bill), then work out the ratio of his orders to his salary by dividing the order value (in £) by his salary. Take care that the order value is 310,000 euros (not 310) and that you should convert to £ before calculating the ratio.

4 Answer **e** £17,000 is correct. Complete the missing information in the 'average order values' for both lists. NB Ensure that you convert the export figures to £000s. Find the highest and lowest values, take the lowest from the highest,

i.e. £21,000 (Pete) − £4000 (Bill) = £17000

5 Answer **a** 110% is correct. Here you must take care to locate the two correct figures to work with, i.e. one salary from each table, then use the formula to calculate the percentage change.

6 Answer **c** £4000 is correct. This requires you to compare the average order value of John and Sue and to state the difference. Note that the answer will be in £000s.

7 Answer **e** 81% is correct. This takes figures for the table and requires you to carry out a number of operations on them. The calculations will be: (total export salaries = £111,000 ÷ 3 = £37,000) – (total UK salaries = £102,100 ÷ 5 = £20,420) = £16,580, then (£16,580 ÷ £20,420) × 100 gives you the percentage difference.

8 Answer **d** 57:92 is correct. This is a straightforward ratio but you must remember that your answer must be in the same order as the question, and also that you are comparing the figures for the averages and these must be calculated first by adding up the two departments and dividing by the number in that department.

9 Answer **b** £361,000 is correct. This one is easy – if you follow the instruction to omit the top two UK representatives and remember that the answer will be in £000s.

10 Answer **a** 9.75% is correct. First find the total amount of orders received and then the difference between that and the target. Then use the familiar formula to find the percentage difference. If you are still finding this type of percentage question at all difficult, commit the following formula to memory:

$$\% \text{ change} = \frac{\text{actual change}}{\text{original whole}} \times 100\%$$

This next set of questions combines two pie charts containing different aspects of information about the same subject. It also tests a combination of skills. A quick glance will tell you that you will be working with percentages (as is often the case when pie charts are used to display data) and as you work through the questions, you will be tested on your ability to add, subtract, multiply and divide. This test is also designed to test your ability to work logically and to understand the information supplied. At face value the pie charts just contain information about the percentages of types of staff and about the length of service in an organisation. However, by combining the two charts and by the addition of one more piece of information – the total number of staff – there is a great deal of information that can be gleaned, and it is this that the questions will require you to find.

11 Answer **c** 33 is correct. Your first step here should be to work out the numbers of administrative and production staff based on the percentages of the total number of staff. Jot down your answers in case you need to use them in the questions to come. Take the number of administrative staff from the number of production staff to get your answer, i.e. 154 − 121 = 33.

12 Answer **e** Cannot say is correct. As there is no category in the length of service pie chart that details 10 to 20 years' service, it is impossible to work out the number in such a category. Do not be afraid of selecting this answer. It is just as important to be able to say what information is not available as it is to be able to use information that is available.

13 Answer **b** 29 is correct. This question demands that you use information from both pie charts to arrive at your answer. First find how many people are in the category, i.e. 24% of 275 = 66. Now, split this number into the same proportions as shown for administrative staff and production staff as shown in the other pie chart, i.e. calculate 44% of 66.

14 Answer **a** 110 is correct. This is a complex question, which will be easier if you break it down into its component parts. First find the percentage of production staff in the two groups (0 to 5 group = 8% (half of 16%) plus 36+ group = 8%, 8 + 8 = 16%), then calculate the number of production staff in these two groups (16% of 275 = 44). Having calculated the total number of production staff when you were doing the first question in this section, you can now complete the calculation by subtracting 44 from 154 (the total number of production staff) to get your answer of 110.

15 Answer **c** 186 is correct. The calculations involved in this question are straightforward but you do need to be careful that you understand what is being asked and that you use the correct figures. Note that one part of the question – the staff leaving the production department – is expressed as a percentage, while the other part – the staff leaving the administration department – is stated as an actual number. You therefore need to work out the number of leavers from the production department (77) and then add the number of administrative staff leaving (12). You will then have 89 leavers and this must be deducted from the total number of staff to get the number of staff remaining.

For the next five questions you are again being asked to combine two different sets of information to find out the answers to the questions. Sometimes you will need to decide where the required data is to be found and for other questions you will need to extract information from both Table 2.3 and Figure 2.3.

16 Answer **d** 6.0% is correct. Here it is only necessary to use the chart showing staff numbers. Find the figures for total staff numbers in Years 1 and 3 then use the formula for % change:

$$\% \text{ change} = \frac{\text{actual change}}{\text{original whole}} \times 100\%$$

17 Answer **e** Product group E is correct. This question requires you to combine the data from Table 2.3 with that in Figure 2.3. Questions like this can appear complicated but if broken down into the different calculations necessary to arrive at an answer, none of them are difficult. The most important phrase in the question is 'sales results per sales person' so, concentrating on Year 2 you should first of all work this out. Step one is to note against each product group, in the column for Year 2, in Table 2.3, the number of sales staff. Now divide each product group's sales figures by the number of sales staff. e.g. Group A = 1,560 ÷12 = 130 and so on. A simple comparison of the five resulting figures will show you the product group with the highest sales results per sales person.

18 Answer **d** Product group D is correct. This question is asking you to look at trends, i.e. a general tendency or direction. It would be advisable to start with product groups D and E as these both show a general direction – one rising steadily over the three years and the other falling consistently. These are definite trends so it is likely to be one of these two product groups. The sales figures for product group D rise steadily from 2,360 to 2,830 to 3,120 whereas those for product group E go up then down. The trend for D therefore is closest to its staff numbers but E does not share the trend.

19 Answer **c** £923,500 is correct. Again you should break this question down into its component parts. First find the average total sales per person in Year 3 (i.e. over all product groups) then multiply by seven. Note that the question only asks 'how much greater' the total sales for that year would be, so do not add your answer on to the total sales figure. The calculation would therefore be total sales for Year 3 divided by the total number of sales staff multiplied by the number of new sales people, i.e. (£11,610,000 ÷ 88) × 7 = £923,500.

20 Answer **c** £215,000 is correct. This question must be tackled methodically. Go through the question locating and noting each piece of information as it is mentioned, then the calculation is as follows: sales in Year 3 ÷ number of sales staff, i.e. 860 ÷ 4. Your answer, of course, will be in £000s.

The remaining five questions in this test use a line diagram (Figure 2.4). These are used to display trends and to compare similar figures from different sources. You must read figures from the graph to get the information for your answers. As with all graphs and charts, you must take care that you note the information in the key.

21 Answer **d** £661,000 is correct. Labour is obviously the greatest expenditure here and you must read off the values for each year then add them together. The exact figure for the year 2004 is £131,000 and if you are in any doubt, let the choice of answers given guide you. Do not forget that the answer will be in £000s as stated on the diagram.

22 Answer **d** 25% is correct. The total expenditure in 2002 was £320,000 and property rent in that year amounted to £80,000. If you spot that 80 is exactly a quarter of 320, then the answer of 25% is easy to find. Otherwise, you will have to calculate by dividing 80 by 320 then multiplying by 100.

23 Answer **a** 137.5% is correct. Before using the formula for calculating the percentage increase, you should assess the figures. With business rates in 2006 costing more than twice as much as in 2002, it will be obvious to you that you should expect an answer in excess of 100% increase. Calculate using the formula:

$$\% \text{ change} = \frac{\text{actual change}}{\text{original whole}} \times 100\%$$

24 Answer **e** £44,000 is correct. Here you simply need to add together the amounts spent on electricity then on water over the period and then subtract one from the other, i.e.

$229 - 185 = 44$. Do not forget that your answer will be in £000s. It can be a good idea to jot down your answers where you have to do separate calculations like this as it may save you time on a subsequent question.

25 Answer **a** £125,000 is correct. In 2002 £320,000 was spent whereas in 2006 a total of £445,000 was spent. It is then a simple matter to subtract one from the other.

TEST 4

1 Answer **b** 30 minutes is correct. Here you are comparing the same journey on different days. You should subtract the time taken on a Monday (1 hour 40 minutes) from the time on Sunday (2 hours 10 minutes).

2 Answer **d** 2 hours 10 minutes is correct. Add 20 minutes to the length of the weekday journey between the two stations – it is irrelevant where the delay is.

3 Answer **e** 14.55 is correct. Add the Sunday journey time on to the new departure time.

4 Answer **b** 2 hours 55 minutes is correct. This is straightforward if you ensure that you are looking at the correct day and stations.

5 Answer **c** 34 hours 10 minutes is correct. Work out the standard weekday journey time and multiply by 2 (to get the return journey time) and by 2 again (because he goes twice every day), then multiply by 4 (he works on each of 4 days during the week), then add on the Sunday journey time multiplied by 2 (as it is a return trip).

6 Answer **c** 3 hours 50 minutes is correct. Find the journey time between the relevant stations on a Sunday then multiply by 2 as it is a return journey.

7 Answer **b** 2 hours 15 minutes is correct.

8 Answer **d** 16.50 is correct. Add 1 hour 10 minutes on to the original arrival time given in the table.

9 Answer **b** 09.30 is correct. The 09.30 train on Saturday from Chesterford was scheduled to arrive at Whitebank at 09.45. If this is brought forward by 15 minutes, this would give a new arrival time of 09.30.

10 Answer **c** 20 hours 40 minutes is correct. The calculation is 45 minutes (Monday to Friday, Whitebank to Neartown) × 5 (5 days) × 4 (journeys per day) = 15 hours. Then calculate 1 hour 25 minutes (Saturday, Whitebank to Middletown) × 4 (number of journeys) = 5 hours 40 minutes. Then 15 hours + 5 hours 40 minutes = 20 hours 40 minutes.

Another pie chart (Figure 2.5) for the next ten questions, but this time you should note that, as stated, the figures shown on the pie chart relate to actual numbers rather than percentages of entrants. Other than that, this is a standard sort of pie chart.

11 Answer **e** 120 is correct. Simply add together all the figures around the perimeter of the 'pie' as these represent the examination entrants.

12 Answer **d** 21% is correct. There were 25 people in the group scoring 41–50% and 120 people in the whole exam group. You therefore need to express 25 as a percentage of 120.

13 Answer **e** Cannot tell is correct. This question shows the limitation of the information presented in this way. To answer this question accurately – and you are not expected to estimate this answer – you would need to know how many people would be in the group 51–55. You do not know the distribution of the 20 people in the group obtaining scores of 51–60 (i.e. how many gained scores of 51 to 55 and how many obtained scores of over 55) and cannot therefore answer the question.

14 Answer **a** 20 is correct. The scores between 21 and 50 cover three score groups. To answer this question you must add together all the people with scores falling in these three groups, i.e. $5 + 20 + 25 = 50$ then select the answer that represents those who passed, i.e. 40% of the entrants.

15 Answer **d** 7 is correct. Here you need to express 8 (the number of entrants with scores in the top bracket of 91–100) as a percentage of 120 (the total number of entrants). You should note that the question is looking for an approximate answer. The actual answer worked out on your calculator will be 6.666 recurring so round this up to 7%.

16 Answer **c** 4 is correct. First find out how many people obtained scores of 51 or over (62). You should not need to add up the other five score groups as you already have the total number of entrants from the first question, so calculate as follows: $62 - (120 - 62) = 4$.

17 Answer **d** 52 is correct. You already know that 62 entrants obtained results in the top half of the scores so you simply need to calculate 62 as a percentage of 120. A shortcut here is to estimate your answer as a little more than a half of the entrants so the only possible answer from the choices given is 52.

18 Answer **a** 58 is correct. Hopefully you will have noted this answer when working out an earlier question. If not, simply add together the actual numbers of people who fall in the relevant five groups.

19 Answer **c** 5 is correct. You will see from the pie chart that 8 people fell into the top group while only 3 were in the bottom group. Subtract the bottom group from the top group to get your answer.

20 Answer **c** 50% is correct. Three groups are relevant to this question and you can see quite clearly that these are half of the pie. If you have time to check, you should locate the relevant groups and add them together, i.e. 25 + 20 + 15 = 60. Then, note that the question asks for a percentage. 60 is, of course, 50% of the total group of 120.

The next ten questions in these timed tests use a column chart (Figure 2.6).

21 Answer **c** £49 is correct. Add together the three remaining cost areas for this product. Electricity 25 + packaging 6 + raw materials 18.

22 Answer **a** £172 is correct. Here you must add together the values in the labour costs column for all five products.

23 Answer **a** £82 is correct. Locate the correct products and columns and then be sure to multiply by two.

24 Answer **c** £139 is correct. It is obvious that products B, C and E are not in the running for this so just tot up the totals of columns for products A and D and select the highest total.

25 Answer **b** Product B is correct. Work out the total production costs for each product. Be sure to write these totals down as they may come in handy for later questions.

26 Answer **e** £79 is correct. Subtract £60 (least expensive = product B) from £139 (most expensive = product D).

27 Answer **d** £3440 is correct. Multiply the total labour costs by five (to give costs for 500) and then by four (number of weeks), i.e. 172 × 5 × 4 = 3440.

28 Answer **b** £130 is correct. The second highest area of costs is electricity and the total of all the columns showing electricity is £130.

29 Answer **a** £25 is correct. First find the average raw material costs of the existing products (18 + 19 + 4 + 45 + 23 = 109 divided by 5 = 21.5), then increase this by 15% to get the approximate costs of the raw materials for the new product.

30 Answer **d** £54 is correct. The production costs for this product this year total £60. A 10% decrease would take this to £54.

Another line diagram (Figure 2.7) for the remaining questions in this test.

31 Answer **b** 10% is correct. This question involves only percentages so you can read directly from the diagram.

32 Answer **c** 0 is correct. The line stayed at a constant level (30%) during these years, i.e. no change in the number of households.

33 Answer **a** PC is correct. Access to a PC increased from 25% to 60%, i.e. 35% increase.

34 Answer **d** 50 is correct. Access to a telephone increased from 85% to 90%, i.e. from 850 households to 900.

35 Answer **e** 35% is correct. To calculate this answer you need to work out the number of households with use of a second car in 2006 (30% of 1000 = 300), add 50 to this then express as a percentage of 1000.

36 Answer **b** 350 is correct. 60% of households had use of a PC in 2006, i.e. 600 households. Subtract from this the number in 2002 (250).

37 Answer **e** 300 is correct. In 2006 900 households had use of a telephone, while 600 had use of a PC. Simply subtract one from the other.

38 Answer **d** Telephone and one car is correct. Both these items increased by just 5%.

39 Answer **e** Cannot tell is correct. There is no information given in the diagram about the overlap in access to the items.

40 Answer **d** 600 is correct. The highest is a telephone at 80%, i.e. 800 households. Subtract the lowest, a second car at 20% = 200 households, to get the answer.

QUANTITATIVE RELATIONS

This type of test relies on your ability to use numbers algebraically and is used as part of the Fast Stream Qualifying Tests for the Civil Service in the United Kingdom. Quantitative relations questions test your reasoning and deductive capabilities when using numbers and also your ability to manipulate data. These skills are useful in many areas in business.

Algebra involves the use of letters to represent numbers. It follows exactly the same rules as arithmetic and uses the same symbols ($+$, $-$, $\times$ and $\div$). Formulae from which you are trying to find the value of a letter (it could be X or, as here, A, B or C) are like a balance or set of scales so that whatever you do to one side of the equation or formula, you must also do to the other side to keep it in balance.

Here is an easy formula to demonstrate this balance effect:

$$A + 8 = 10$$

Now, just one glance will tell you that A must equal 2 but how did we solve this formula?

The method is firstly to isolate the item that we are trying to find by removing the 8 from the left-hand side. To keep the balance we must also remove 8 from the right-hand side:

$$A + 8 - 8 = 10 - 8$$

and this is equivalent to:

$$A = 2$$

If there is a coefficient (a number by which the unknown letter is multiplied) on one side of the equation you should divide both sides by that coefficient. This keeps it balanced. For example:

$$2A = 10$$

divide both sides by 2:

$$A = 10 \div 2$$

therefore $A = 5$.

The formulae in these tests are quite basic and use only three letters as a substitute for numbers. Algebra used in this way involves relationships – you need to find the numerical relationship between the figures in each row and the easiest way to express this relationship – or pattern – is by using an algebraic expression.

Your task in this type of question is to find the formula that applies to all the rows of numbers in the question. This will then allow you to find the missing number in the final row. You can do this by studying the first four rows to find a pattern. You must express this pattern as a formula that can then be applied to the final row to find the missing number. The way that you must indicate your answers in this type of test is very specific. You should follow the instructions very carefully. Any deviation from this may result in your answer being marked as incorrect.

TEST 5

1 The answer is 31 and the formula is $A + B = C$. This is a simple formula to start this section and is a sequence that you should find easy to spot, i.e. in the first row $2 + 3 = 5$, in the second row $7 + 8 = 15$ and so on until the final row $8 + 23 = ?$ must give the answer 31.

2 The answer is 24 and the formula is $A - B = C$. This is another straightforward formula but you have to find the number at the beginning of the row so you will need to restate the formula to read $A = B + C$.

3 The answer is 12 and the formula is $3A - C = B$. That is, subtract C (3) from $3 \times A$ (15) to give the answer.

4 The answer is 10 and the formula is $A - B = 2C$. You will find this easier if you restate the relationship as $(C \times 2) + B = A$, i.e. $(4 \times 2) + 2 = 10$.

5 The answer is 7 and the formula is $A \div B = C$. The previous questions have involved addition and subtraction and now division is being introduced. The calculations are not difficult and the key to success is in spotting the relationship between the three columns.

6 The answer is 4 and the formula is $3A \div B = C$. Division again but also multiplication in that the figures in column A must be multiplied by 3 then divided by the figure in column B to get the answer C.

7 The answer is 4 and the formula is $2A - B = C$. The way to spot the pattern is to ask yourself what needs to be done to the figures in the first two columns to get the figure in the third column. In this case you must double the number in the first column then subtract the figure in column B to get the number in column C.

8 The answer is 11 and the formula is $A + 2B = C$. Another way to state this relationship so that it shows A as the part of the formula that you must find is $C - 2B = A$. You will note that by changing which side of the formula one of the figures is stated, you must also change the mathematical operation to be performed, i.e. from plus to minus.

TEST 6

1 The answer is 20 and the formula is $B - A = 2C$. To find the figure in column B in the final row, restate the relationship as $B = 2C + A$.

2 The answer is 56 and the formula is $A \times (2B) = C$. Here you should work through each row finding out what must be done with the numbers in columns A and B to arrive at the figure in column C. As all the figures in column C are significantly higher than both the figures in columns A and B, you should look for an element of multiplication. In the first row, it could be either A or B that should be multiplied by itself as these figures are the same but when you move on to the next row or two you can see that B is multiplied by itself before being multiplied by A to get your answer, C.

3 The answer is 30 and the formula is $A + 2B = C$. If you take the value of A away from C in each row, the resulting number is twice the value of B. Therefore, on the final row, $18 + (6 \times 2) = 30$.

4 The answer is 32 and the formula is $A - B = C$. This is more straightforward and gets even easier if you restate the relationship as $A = B + C$, i.e. $A = 3 + 29 = 32$.

5 The answer is 17 and the formula is $2A - B = C$. As you are looking for B in the final row, it will again be helpful to restate the formula as $B = 2A - C$.

6 The answer is 45 and the formula is $B - A = 2C$. If you take the value of A from the value of B you will get a figure that is twice the value of C, i.e. in the final row this would be calculated as $95 - 5 = 90$, $90 \div 2 = 45$.

7 The answer is 2 and the formula is $A \times (2B) = C$. The key to finding the relationship between the numbers in the three columns here is finding what you have to do to the number in column A to arrive at the number in column C, e.g. in the first row A (5) must be multiplied by 8 to get 40 (C). Then you can see how 8 relates to B – it is twice the value of B.

8 The answer is 16 and the formula is A ÷ B = C. Working with the figures in the first four rows, if you divide the value of A by the value of B, you will arrive at C. So, to find A, as in this case, you should restate this as A = B × C.

TEST 7

1 The answer is 16 and the formula is A − B = 2C. Here, as in many of these questions it may help you to look at the general direction of the numbers from right to left. That is, do they go up or down and is this rise or fall a steep one or are the figures close to one another? In this case, the numbers decrease sharply and this could signify an element of multiplication in the formula. Here by deducting B (4) from A (36), you get the value of two Cs (32) so halve this to get your answer.

2 The answer is 10 and the formula is 2A ÷ B = C. Here both multiplication and division are involved as the relationship is (2 × A) ÷ B = C. As usual when solving algebra questions, you should isolate the unknown figure on one side of the formula. This would give you B = 2A ÷ C, i.e. (25 × 2) ÷ 5 = 10.

3 The answer is 7 and the formula is B − A = 3C. Again, the values decrease from right to left so you should look for the multiplier. If you subtract the value of A (6) from B (27) you get C × 3 so divide by 3 to get your answer of 7.

4 The answer is 6 and the formula is A + 2B = C. Restate this as 2B = C − A so that if you subtract 8 from 20 you get 12 and as this is 2 × B you must halve this to get the correct value of B.

5 The answer is 3 and the formula is $2A + B = C$. As you are looking for the value of B in this question, it will be helpful to restate this as $B = C - 2A$, i.e. $39 - (2 \times 18) = 3$.

6 The answer is 7 and the formula is $C - B = A \div 2$. If you take the value of B (7) away from C (21) the resulting number is twice the value of A, i.e. $21 - 7 = 14$, and $14 \div 2 = 7$.

7 The answer is 18 and the formula is $A \times (2B) = C$. To find C you must multiply double the value of B by the value of A, i.e. $C = (2 \times 3) \times 3 = 18$.

8 The answer is 3 and the formula is $C \div B = A + 1$. That is C (16) divided by the value of B (4) gives you the value of A plus 1. This is perhaps a more difficult formula to find as it involves division as well as a 'value plus one' but you should follow the same approach of finding the relationship of the numbers in the first four rows and then apply it to the fifth row.

TEST 8

1 The answer is 4 and the formula is $(A + 1) - B = 2C$. When you deduct the value of B (2) from $A + 1$ $(9 + 1)$, you get two Cs so you should halve it to get your answer.

2 The answer is 9 and the formula is $A + 2B = C$. Here you are looking for the value of B. As $2B = C - A$, the calculation will be $(23 - 5) \div 2 = 9$.

3 The answer is 8 and the formula is $A + 2B = C + 1$. Restate this as $A = (C + 1) - (B \times 2)$ then substitute the figures that you know to give $A = (25 + 1) - (9 \times 2) = 26 - 18 = 8$.

4 The answer is 28 and the formula is A ÷ B = C. To find the value of A you should work out C × B = A so that using the figures form the final row you will have 2 × 14 = 28.

5 The answer is 8 and the formula is A − B = 2C. Here you must subtract the value of B (18) from the value of A (34) to give you 2C. Divide this by two to give you the value of C.

6 The answer is 8 and the formula is A + B = C ÷ 2. To find the missing figure, i.e. the value of A in the final row, you could restate the relationship as A = (C ÷ 2) − B.

7 The answer is 9 and the formula is A + 3B = 2C. When you calculate A (6) plus 3B (4 × 3) you will arrive at a figure that is twice the value of C so halve it to get your answer.

8 The answer is 25 and the formula is (A + 1) − 2B = 2C. This is a difficult question to end this section so if you get to this point you can spend the remaining time allowed on this one without worrying that you are neglecting an easier question. You are trying to find A and the figures in the A row all have one added to their value before being used in the formula. The relationship can be restated as A = (2B + 2C) − 1, i.e. (8 × 2) + (5 × 2) − 1 = 16 + 10 − 1 = 25.

TEST 9

1 The answer is 4 and the formula is A − B = 2C. When you subtract B (3) from A (11), you will get a figure that is twice the value of C so halve it to get the answer.

2 The answer is 3 and the formula is (A + 1) − B = 2C. Here you are trying to find the value of B so it may help to restate the question as B = (A + 1) − 2C.

3 The answer is 14 and the formula is A ÷ B = C. This relationship could also be stated as C × B = A, so you can find the value of A by multiplying C (7) by B (2).

4 The answer is 99 and the formula is B − A = 2C. The figures in the final row of this question are larger than in previous questions but this should not deter you. If you isolate B on one side of the formula (B = 2C + A), it is a simple calculation.

5 The answer is 14 and the formula is A + 2B = C. First look at the relationship of A to the two known values, then subtract two Bs (8 × 2) from the value of C (30), and you will find the value of A (14).

6 The answer is 6 and the formula is C ÷ B = A + 1. If you divide the value of C (21) by B (3), the resulting figure is A + 1 so subtract one to get the correct value for A.

7 The answer is 14 and the formula is B − A = 2C. If you subtract the value of A (8) from B (14), the result is twice the value of C (3).

8 The answer is 15 and the formula is 2A − (B + 1) = C. By subtracting the value of B + 1 (6 + 1) from the value of 2A (11 × 2), you will arrive at the value of C (15).

TEST 10

1 The answer is 3 and the formula is 3A − C = B. If you multiply the value of A (10) by 3 and subtract the value of C (27) you will arrive at the value of B (3).

2 The answer is 4 and the formula is A + B = C. This is probably the simplest formula and is one that should be apparent to you immediately.

3 The answer is 11 and the formula is A + 3B = 2C. If you multiply the value of B by 3 then add it to A, the answer will be twice the value of C.

4 The answer is 61 and the formula is A − B = 2C. To find B you could restate the relationship as B = A − 2C so that by deducting twice the value of C from the value of A you obtain the value of B.

5 The answer is 40 and the formula is C ÷ B = A + 1. Another way to show this relationship is (A + 1) × B = C, i.e. (4 + 1) × 8 = 40.

6 The answer is 24 and the formula is A ÷ B = C. You may also have noticed that the values in column C (all are 3) multiplied by the values in column B give you the values in column A.

7 The answer is 6 and the formula is 2A + B = C + 1. This is the same as (C + 1) − B = 2A so (14 + 1) − 3 = 12; which is twice the value of A.

8 The answer is 2 and the formula is 2A − B = C. By deducting the value of C (36) from twice the value of A (19 × 2) you will arrive at the value of B (2).

TEST 11

1 The answer is 100 and the formula is A × (2B) = C. If you multiply A (10) by twice the value of B (5 × 2), you will get the value of C (100).

2 The answer is 9 and the formula is 2A − (B + 1) = C. To find A you should calculate (3 + 1 + 14) ÷ 2 = 9.

3 The answer is 13 and the formula is $A + 2B = C + 1$. Find A by deducting one from the value of C then subtracting the value of two Bs from this.

4 The answer is 10 and the formula is $C - B = A \div 2$. If you divide A (16) by two and add the value of B you will get the value of C.

5 The answer is 3 and the formula is $A - B = 2C$. If you subtract B (?) from A (9), the result is the value of two Cs (3×2), i.e. you must subtract 3.

6 The answer is 20 and the formula is $3A - C = B$. Three times the value of A (8×3) less the value of C (20) will give you the value of B (4).

7 The answer is 6 and the formula is $A + 2B = C$. Restate the relationship as $A = C - (B \times 2)$, i.e. $36 - 30 = 6$.

8 The answer is 3 and the formula is $A + 3B = 2C$. To find A, calculate 2C (15×2) $-$ 3B (9×3).

TEST 12

1 The answer is 80 and the formula is $C \div B = A + 1$. To arrive at the value of C, you need to add one to the value of A and then multiply by B, i.e. $(3 + 1) \times 20 = 80$.

2 The answer is 4 and the formula is $A + B = C \div 2$. Restate this relationship as $B = (C \div 2) - A$ and the calculation is then $B = (208 \div 2) - 100 = 4$.

3 The answer is 4 and the formula is $(A + 1) - B = 2C$. If you add one to the value of A ($14 + 1$) then deduct B (7) you will get a figure that is twice the value of C so divide by two to get the correct value.

4 The answer is 4 and the formula is $3A - C = 2B$. This relationship can be restated as $C = 3A - 2B$. Multiply A by 3 (8×3) and take away twice the value of B (2×10) to get the value of C (4).

5 The answer is 8 and the formula is $B - A = 2C$. If you multiply the value of C by 2 and add the value of A you will arrive at the value of B.

6 The answer is 5 and the formula is $(A + 1) - B = C$. Add one to the value of A then subtract B to find the value of C.

7 The answer is 26 and the formula is $A - 2B = 2C$. An alternative way of showing this relationship is $(B + C) \times 2 = A$. You can therefore add B and C together before multiplying the product of this calculation by two to get the value of A.

8 The answer is 37 and the formula is $2A + B = C$. By multiplying the value of A by 2 then adding the value of B you will arrive at the value of C.

TEST 13

This test is made up of a mixture of all the different types of questions that you will find in this book and the first 12 questions are based on general arithmetic. For some questions you may use a calculator while for others you may not. Don't be tempted to speed up the process by using your calculator for all the questions in this mixed test, as you will be missing out on valuable practice. If you have had any problems with these first 12 questions, look back at the first section in this chapter for a few tips on how to tackle questions of this type.

Now let's look at explanations for each question:

1 The answer is 502. Providing you deal with the calculation within the brackets separately (14.4 × 2 = 28.8) and then insert the answer into the rest of the problem, you should have no problem with this. It would then be 477 + 29.2 + 28.8 − 33 = 502.

2 The answer is 20. Again, deal with the brackets first, then continue with the calculation.

3 The answer is 21,052. This is a straightforward calculation that you should take time over to be sure of getting it right.

The next three questions involve estimating your answers.

4 Answer **c** 57 is correct. The easiest way to tackle this question is to round up the 29 to 30 then quickly divide it into 1650. This gives you 55 and there is only one answer that is close to this.

5 Answer **a** 75 is correct. Again, a bit of rounding up will help. Round up 29.6 to 30 and multiply by two and a half times. This gives you 75, which is an approximate answer to the question so choose that from the answers given.

6 Answer **e** 49,900 is correct. Here you're mixing decimals with fractions but it is straightforward. A half is 0.5 so adding it to 49.4 gives you nearly 50. Add three zeros and you have something close to the correct answer.

Next come three word problems. The skill here is in picking out the relevant bits of information and using them to calculate your answer.

7 Answer **d** £550,559 is correct. First work out 10% of £18,500 (by deleting a zero) then putting that into the calculation i.e 575,655 − 23,246 − 1850 = 550,559. NB As there are two answers very close to each other, you must be precise − estimating would not help you here.

8 Answer **c** 12 is correct. This is a simple calculation so long as you ensure you use the correct figures for men and for women − in the question they are in different orders.

9 Answer **d** £8,173,151 is correct. Here you simply find a sixth of the current year's amount and add it on to the current year to get your answer.

Now we're moving on in this mixed test to number sequences. Look back to page 123 for advice on working with this type of problem if you find any of them difficult.

10 Answer **c** 17.8 is correct. Each number in the sequence is multiplied by 0.75.

11 Answer **a** 67 is correct. The pattern of the gaps between the numbers is +4, +2, +4, +2 and so on.

12 Answer **e** 92.9 is correct. If you jot down the differences between each pair of numbers you will easily see that the sequence here is −1.8, +1, −1.8, +1 and so on.

Now we move on to using information supplied in pie charts. Work methodically with these questions and you should have no problems. Read the question carefully, deciding which chart will give you the information required.

13 Answer **c** 25 million is correct. Find the region with the largest number of stores then concentrate on extracting information about this from the chart that gives you details of customer transactions.

14 Answer **e** £672.5 million is correct. This simply requires you to add the retail sales values for all regions together.

15 Answer **a** 354 is correct. Find the total number of stores in each of the regions mentioned then deduct one figure from the other to get your answer.

16 Answer **e** 35,714 is correct. Here you're asked to calculate an average figure. Divide the total sales in the Middle East by the number of stores in that region.

17 Answer **a** £435,000 is correct. First you'll need to work out the total number of stores and the total sales value for the group then divide to get your answer.

In the final two questions in this test you have to use algebraic formulae to find the answer. If you find these difficult, look back to the explanation of quantitative relations and algebra on pages 143–145.

18 The answer is 9 and the formula is $(A + 1) - B = 3C$.

19 The answer is 180 and the formula is $2A \times B = C$.

CHAPTER FOUR
DIAGNOSIS AND
FURTHER READING

DIAGNOSIS

There is no way for you to know, before you start, how the test will be scored. However, your score will be standardised relative to those of other candidates in your peer group.

Some tests allow use of a calculator, some award points for completing more questions, others may deduct points for incorrect answers. There are many variables about these tests and it is therefore vital that you read the instructions carefully.

Scores are usually calculated using a percentile scoring system. This is why the final number of answers you have given correctly does not necessarily translate directly into a percentage score but into a percentile rating relative to a known distribution. A basic scoring system is shown here so that you can score your answers and get an idea of your aptitude for this subject.

Each question that you have answered correctly scores 5 marks as follows:

Correct answers	1	2	3	4	5	6	7	8	9	10	11	12
	5	10	15	20	25	30	35	40	45	50	55	60

For each question that you did not attempt, deduct 2 marks from your final 'correct marks' score as follows:

Questions not attempted	1	2	3	4	5	6	7	8	9	10	11	12
Deducted marks	2	4	6	8	10	12	14	16	18	20	22	24

For example, 36 questions correct, 2 incorrect, 2 not attempted, would score as follows:

36 correct $\times$ 5 marks = 180
2 incorrect $\times$ 0 marks = 0
2 incomplete $\times$ -2 = -4

'Raw' test score = $180 - 4 = 176$

NB Each test will have a potential score according to the number of questions in that particular test, of course.

You will have a separate score for each of the tests – do not add these together but use them to chart your progress as you go through the book.

Now use the following chart according to the number of questions in the tests to interpret your final score for each test:

Number of questions in test	Well below average	Below average	Average	Above average	Well above average
25	0 to 35	36 to 59	60 to 75	76 to 104	105 or over
32	0 to 40	41 to 85	86 to 100	101 to 130	131 or over
40	0 to 50	51 to 99	100 to 125	126 to 164	165 or over

You will notice that your score has not been given in percentage terms as this is not relevant when assessing your performance in tests of this type. The important thing to understand is your score relative to those of other candidates in your peer group.

If your score is 'Above average' or 'Well above average', you may decide that you would like to spend more of your preparation time on other sections of the tests you may sit – maybe verbal reasoning, or diagrammatic reasoning. If the results indicate that your score is 'Average' or below, get some help with the basics of numeracy before your test.

Whatever your score, do not allow yourself to be discouraged – tests are only part of the interview process and it is possible to improve with practice.

HOW WILL AN EMPLOYER ASSESS AND USE THE RESULTS OF THESE TESTS?

The person conducting the tests will mark and interpret them according to a pre-set marking scheme. Different test-setters and employers may have their own, quite complex, marking schemes and it is therefore impossible to predict final scores. Indeed, your actual score is not important in itself. It is important to note that your test will be marked against a norm – this may be scores gained by previous applicants or by people at different management levels. The main point is that they are standard tests – everyone is given the same questions and instructions, the same amount of time to answer and they are all assessed according to a standard marking system. This is so that scores can be compared and interpreted. When you take a psychometric test, you will be compared with your peers, that is with the people with whom you are competing for a job. Yes, this is a competition – and we want to help you to win!

MARKING SCHEMES

When the test publishers – the people who devise the tests – check the effectiveness of the tests by using it with large numbers of people, they will develop 'norm' tables. They then work out what will be an average score and what will be above or below average taking into account the interviewee's age, sex, education and so on. Employers use these norm tables to assist them in evaluating performance in the tests. They help in assessing the potential of the candidate to do the job in question.

When employers are testing a large number of people, they may introduce a cut-off point and, for example, take scorers in the top 10 per cent. Alternatively, they may have a target score in mind and take anyone who reaches this score for further assessment or interview. Another way in which employers may decide to use the results from psychometric tests is to help them to whittle down a large number of applicants into a more manageable group by eliminating candidates who score below a certain number of correct answers.

It should be noted here that some marking schemes use what is known as 'negative scoring'. That is to say that you will have your score reduced for every incorrect answer. If that is the case in a test that you find yourself sitting, do not be tempted to guess the answers. Accuracy, not estimation, is the name of the game if negative scoring is used.

WHAT DO THE TESTS PROVE?

When used and selected correctly, this sort of test will help to prove – or disprove – your suitability for the job in question. If employers have decided that a certain job requires particular competencies and aptitudes then that is what they must test for. Of course, their assumptions about the job requirements may be wrong but there is little that can be done about this. For this reason the results of aptitude tests like this should not be viewed as 'pass' or 'fail'. The test is more an exercise in exploring where you will be best suited. There is little point in getting a job that would be wrong for you – that would be counter-productive for you and expensive for the employer.

SUGGESTIONS FOR FURTHER IMPROVEMENT

THE VALUE OF PREPARATION

It has been proved that everyone can improve his or her test scores by practising. Unfamiliarity gets in the way of your natural ability, so practice is an invaluable form of preparation. Olympic runners do not just turn up at the track and set off as fast as they can – they will practise, treat their mind and body well and find out all they can about the race. Why should taking any other sort of test be different? So make the most of your period of preparation. Practice – with questions similar to those that you will meet in your tests – is the most important element of your preparation strategy. It will help you to revise the things you learned at school and to improve your test technique. The timed tests in Chapter 2 will help you to become familiar with the test formats and how to tackle the variety of questions that you may face. Aim to practise for up to two hours in any one session. Any more than that may be counter-productive. It is almost impossible to sustain the intense concentration needed for much longer than two hours.

But what other forms of preparation should you consider?

Apart from the intensive practice that you can take advantage of by using the timed tests, there are other sorts of practice. For example, you should make yourself aware of the numbers that are all around you – and use them.

- When you are shopping in the supermarket, estimate what your total bill will be or continually calculate how much you can save by buying one product rather than another.

- When you are on a long car journey, use the opportunity to practise a little mental arithmetic. Work out how many more miles to your destination, your average speed, percentage of the journey completed and so on.

- Notice the data that is presented to you everyday in the financial pages of newspapers.

- Seek out numerical information in company reports or in trade magazines.

- Use train timetables to gain familiarity with using information presented in this way.

- Practise using currency exchange rates given in newspapers or by your travel agent.

- Brush up on using fractions, square roots, multiplication tables, percentages and decimals.

- Make sure you can use your calculator efficiently – you will not always be allowed to use one, but be prepared.

Above all, do not be afraid of numbers. If, after doing the tests in this book, you have specific concerns about your mathematical knowledge, get yourself a good, basic maths book and get yourself up to speed. Then practise until you are happy using numbers.

Apart from concentrating your efforts on improving your ability with numbers, you might want to consider other forms of preparation. For example, psychological preparation can be extremely important. Worrying about your interview or your test results will not improve your performance. There are a number of relaxation techniques that can reduce your stress levels and help you to control your anxiety. These include:

- Listening to relaxation tapes
- Meditation
- Yoga
- Hypnotherapy
- Stress counselling
- Positive visualisation
- An exercise regime

Whatever you choose – and it is very much an individual choice – your aim should be to arrive for your test in a calm, controlled state of mind. You need to shut out negative thoughts such as 'I'm hopeless at maths' or 'I can't do tests' and allow extensive practice to increase your confidence. If you can concentrate on positive outcomes you will increase your confidence and calmness.

THE TEST ITSELF

Tests will be timed and not much time will be allowed for you to do the tests – it will be tight – and it is frequently not possible to complete all the tests in the time allotted. Do not let this worry you.

Even when you are sitting in the test room, you can still improve your chances of success. There are a few important things to remember at this stage:

- Listen to – and be sure to comply with – the instructions given by the test administrator.

- Read the instructions on the test paper – these may cover items such as:

  - how much time you will be allowed
  - whether or not you may write on the margins of the test paper or if rough paper is supplied for your workings
  - whether the use of calculators is permitted
  - exactly how you should indicate your answer – with a tick or a cross for example
  - how to make alterations to your answers if necessary

- Work through the questions methodically – do not be tempted to rush on to later questions first. Some papers are structured so that the questions get progressively more difficult – if you look at the later questions first, you may waste time on more difficult questions while throwing away easy points you could have scored on the earlier questions.

- If you do not understand something at this stage – before the test begins – speak up. There are sometimes example questions that you will be instructed to read before the timed test begins. Use the time allowed for this to ensure that you understand exactly what you are being asked to do. Do not try to pretend that you know everything – you do not need to impress the other candidates.

- Read the questions carefully. Although you will be trying to work quickly, there is no point in answering all the questions but getting many of them wrong because you did not understand what was required.

STRATEGY

The main strategy during the test will involve timing – see below – but you may also want to consider how much you will use your powers of estimation. Here again, practice will help. Some questions on a numerical reasoning test are ideal for estimation. Rounding up or down can often be a quick way of arriving at the only possible answer from those given in multiple-choice questions. However, as noted above, take care if a system using negative scoring will be used – then accuracy is really important.

If you are really struggling with a particular question, do not waste time. Finding a difficult question can be unnerving. Far better to move on – there may be later questions that you find easy.

Try not to let people around you affect your performance. Just because the person at the next desk to you has turned over a lot more pages than you, it does not mean that you are doing badly. They might have all their answers wrong!

TIMING

The time allowed for the various numerical tests that you will undertake will range from just a few minutes for an arithmetic test to maybe forty minutes for a test involving charts, tables or algebra. If you are being tested on a number of aptitudes, the testing session may well take up to two hours in total.

The important thing is to use your time wisely. It is rare that too much time will be allowed for a numerical reasoning test. It is far more likely that you will run out of time. You will therefore need to work quickly while trying to be as accurate as possible. Try not to let one question take up too much of your time. If a particular question is proving difficult for you, move on. You could always come back to it if you were to find that you have plenty of time. So keep going steadily right through to the end of the test. You are aiming at a balance between speed and accuracy. It would be unusual for someone to get all the questions right, so it is better to attempt every question and get some wrong than to spend too long on one difficult question and then run out of time, possibly missing out on some easier questions.

Do not forget that, depending on the scoring scheme, there may be penalties applied for incorrect answers or for questions not attempted. You will therefore need to manage your time carefully.

Remember that your own reactions to your performance in the tests are subjective. You are quite often not the best judge of your own performance. It might help you if you can get some feedback about your results from the test administrators. However, this is sometimes difficult to obtain as it is a time-consuming task for employers to undertake.

Above all, keep an open mind. You can improve, and your dislike of maths at school does not have to last for the rest of your life. The obvious incentive for you to undertake all this extra effort is the job you really want and the salary you deserve.

Good luck!

ON THE DAY

You must plan to arrive at the test centre in a state that is conducive to achieving your best possible score. This means being calm and focused. It is possible that you may feel nervous before the test, but you can help yourself by preparing in advance the practical details that will enable you to do well. Remember, it is unlikely that you are the only person who is feeling nervous; what is important is how you deal with your nerves! The following suggestions may help you to overcome unnecessary test-related anxiety.

1 Know where the test centre is located, and estimate how long it will take you to get there – plan your 'setting off time'. Now plan to leave 45 minutes before your setting off time to allow for travel delays. This way, you can be more or less certain that you will arrive at the test centre in good time. If, for any reason, you think you will miss the start of the session, call the administrator to ask for instructions.

2 Try to get a good night's sleep before the test. This is obvious advice and, realistically, it is not always possible, particularly if you are prone to nerves the night before a test. However, you can take some positive steps to help. Consider taking a hot bath before you go to bed, drinking

herbal rather than caffeinated tea, and doing some exercise. Think back to what worked last time you took an exam and try to replicate the scenario.

3 The night before the test, organise everything that you need to take with you. This includes test instructions, directions, your identification, pens, erasers, possibly your calculator (with new batteries in it), reading glasses, and contact lenses.

4 Decide what you are going to wear and have your clothes ready the night before. Be prepared for the test centre to be unusually hot or cold, and dress in layers so that you can regulate the climate yourself. If your test will be preceded or followed by an interview, make sure you dress accordingly for the interview which is likely to be a more formal event than the test itself.

5 Eat breakfast! Even if you usually skip breakfast, you should consider that insufficient sugar levels affect your concentration and that a healthy breakfast might help you to concentrate, especially towards the end of the test when you are likely to be tired.

6 If you know that you have specific or exceptional requirements which will require preparation on the day, be sure to inform the test administrators in advance so that they can assist you as necessary. This may include wheelchair access, the availability of the test in Braille, or a facility for those with hearing difficulties. Similarly, if you are feeling unusually unwell on the day of the test, make sure that the test administrator is aware of it.

7 If, when you read the test instructions, there is something you don't understand, ask for clarification from the administrator. The time given to you to read the instructions may or may not be limited but, within the allowed time, you can usually ask questions. Don't assume that you have understood the instructions if, at first glance, they appear to be similar to the instructions for the practice tests.

8 Don't read through all the questions before you start. This simply wastes time. Start with Question 1 and work swiftly and methodically through each question in order. Unless you are taking a computerised test where the level of difficulty of the next question depends on you correctly answering the previous question (such as the GMAT or GRE), don't waste time on questions that you know require a lot of time. You can return to these questions at the end if you have time left over.

9 After you have taken the test, find out the mechanism for feedback, and approximately the number of days you will have to wait to find out your results. Ask whether there is scope for objective feedback on your performance for your future reference.

10 Celebrate that you have finished.

FURTHER SOURCES OF PRACTICE

In this final section, you will find a list of useful sources for all types of psychometric tests.

BOOKS

Bolles, Richard N., *What Color Is Your Parachute?* Berkeley, CA: Ten Speed Press, 2007.

Carter, P. and K. Russell, *Psychometric Testing: 1000 Ways to Assess Your Personality, Creativity, Intelligence and Lateral Thinking.* Chichester: John Wiley, 2001.

Jackson, Tom, *The Perfect Résumé.* New York: Broadway Books, 2004.

Kourdi, Jeremy, *Succeed at Psychometric Testing: Practice Tests for Verbal Reasoning Advanced.* London: Hodder Education, 2008.

Krannich, Ronald L. and Caryl Rae Krannich, *Network Your Way to Job and Career Success.* Manassa, VA: Impact Publications, 1989.

Nuga, Simbo, *Succeed at Psychometric Testing: Practice Tests for Verbal Reasoning Intermediate.* London: Hodder Education, 2008.

Rhodes, Peter, *Succeed at Psychometric Testing: Practice Tests for Critical Verbal Reasoning.* London: Hodder Education, 2008.

Rhodes, Peter, *Succeed at Psychometric Testing: Practice Tests for Diagrammatic and Abstract Reasoning.* London: Hodder Education, 2008.

Vanson, Sally, *Succeed at Psychometric Testing: Practice Tests for Data Interpretation.* London: Hodder Education, 2008.

Walmsley, Bernice, *Succeed at Psychometric Testing: Practice Tests for Numerical Reasoning Intermediate.* London: Hodder Education, 2008.

Walmsley, Bernice, *Succeed at Psychometric Testing: Practice Tests for the National Police Selection Process.* London: Hodder Education, 2008.

TEST PUBLISHERS AND SUPPLIERS

ASE
Chiswick Centre
414 Chiswick High Road
London W4 5TF
telephone: 0208 996 3337
www.ase-solutions.co.uk

Oxford Psychologists Press
Elsfield Hall
15–17 Elsfield Way
Oxford OX2 8EP
telephone: 01865 404500
www.opp.co.uk

Psytech International Ltd
The Grange
Church Road
Pulloxhill
Bedfordshire MK45 5HE
telephone: 01525 720003
www.psytech.co.uk

SHL
The Pavilion
1 Atwell Place
Thames Ditton
Surrey KT7 0SR
telephone: 0208 398 4170
www.shl.com

The Psychological Corporation
Harcourt Assessment
Halley Court
Jordan Hill
Oxford OX2 8EJ
www.tpc-international.com

The Test Agency Ltd
Burgner House
4630 Kingsgate
Oxford Business Park South
Oxford OX4 2SU
telephone: 01865 402900
www.testagency.com

OTHER USEFUL WEBSITES

Websites are prone to change, but the following are correct at the time of going to press.

www.careerpsychologycentre.com

www.cipd.org.uk

www.deloitte.co.uk/index.asp

www.ets.org

www.freesat1prep.com

www.mensa.org.uk

www.morrisby.co.uk

www.newmonday.co.uk

www.oneclickhr.com

www.pgcareers.com/apply/how/recruitment.asp

www.psychtesting.org.uk

www.psychtests.com

www.publicjobs.gov.ie

www.puzz.com

www.testagency.co.uk

www.tests-direct.com

OTHER USEFUL ORGANISATIONS

American Psychological Association Testing and Assessment – www.apa.org/science/testing

Association of Recognised English Language Schools (ARELS) – www.englishuk.com

Australian Psychological Society – www.psychology.org.au

The Best Practice Club – www.bpclub.com

The British Psychological Society – www.bps.org.uk

Canadian Psychological Association – www.cpa.ca

The Chartered Institute of Marketing – www.cim.co.uk

The Chartered Institute of Personnel and Development – www.cipd.co.uk

The Chartered Management Institute – www.managers.org.uk

Psyconsult – www.psyconsult.co.uk

Singapore Psychological Society – www.singaporepsychologicalsociety.co.uk

Society for Industrial and Organisational Assessment (South Africa) (SIOPSA) – www.siposa.org.za